"GENTLY"
OFF WITH THE LID!

To David

Very best wishes to you & the family. Hopefully
to bring out a smile or two!
David
3/8/07.

DAVID WHITMORE

"Gently" Off with the lid

Also by David Whitmore:
Gently thru' life

Typeset and Published by:

Able Publishing
13 Station Road
Knebworth
Hertfordshire SG3 6AP

Tel: 01438 812320   Fax: 01438 815232

Email: books@ablepublishing.co.uk

Website: www.ablepublishing.co.uk

CONTENTS

INTRODUCTION

This book seeks to 'gently lift the lid' from a special group of people. At first sight they do not seem particularly special in the quick-moving world of today but they all have one thing in common making them the exception – each of them seeks to help the community in their various different ways. All this despite 'the necessary regulations' which for whatever good reason seem to act these days in order to inhibit this kind of initiative.

However it seems in no small part due to their persistence and most of all to their sense of humour which makes the difference in overcoming all obstacles on the way to achieve success. In many cases success means being able to continue organisations for young people despite, as far as leaders are concerned, the much increased difficulty of finding slots for earning a living and keeping a young family.

I would go so far as to say that without this kind of input there would be little left of certain out-of-school activities which remain so essential for the development of our children.

More frighteningly still will be the effect on our army, navy and air force if the band of dedicated ex-servicemen are not prepared to continue to give of their time to introduce young people to service life by means of our various thriving cadet forces. Yes there certainly were many eye openers ready for us as we met some thriving organisations we did not even know existed.

It is for this reason I have concentrated on the fun side of many of the stories connected with the 400 or so engagements we performed on behalf of the Council. Many a tale was well worth the telling!

At the same time I could not resist adding a few anecdotes in connection with the time just prior to this when I was plunged unceremoniously into the sewage industry as the consultant just prior to taking up what I would describe in the other more refined context as the 'velvet mantle of local government.'

I hope you enjoy this quiet read.

David Whitmore

DEDICATION

This book is dedicated to Dr A Al-Niaimi and his special team at mid Staffs General Hospital who day by day under our NHS work towards improving the quality of life of their patients.

ACKNOWLEDGEMENTS

We should like to express our thanks to all who helped us during our mayoral years, to the Clerk and secretaries of the Town Council and more especially to the management and secretaries at the Borough Council, to the council chauffeurs who drove us about and kept us cheerful, to the unpaid volunteers particularly Pamela Anderson who helped with contacts with local schools in Burton, people completely unknown to us at the time.

Thanks also to the local press in both Uttoxeter and Burton, to Graham Phoenix of the Post and Times who allowed me to contribute weekly articles of happenings in Uttoxeter during the first mayoral year and to the Advertiser and Burton Mail group together with Harry Arnold Ltd "Waterways Images" for their support and permission to reproduce their photos. To Cllr Geoff Morrison who took the picture of both of us at the start, to my brother-in-law Martin who attended not a few of our engagements with his camera and certainly not the least to the IWA for permission to use the delightful picture of their unique steam boat *President* with all aboard for the National Waterways festival. Lastly and by no means least to my wife Cynthia and daughter in law Jo who kindly took upon themselves the onerous job of reading the proofs.

THE AUTHOR

D AVID WHITMORE was born into a textile family just before the Second World War and was educated at Nottingham high school and Loughborough Grammar School, finally taking his engineering degree 'in the smoke' at Manchester University in 1961.

He married Cynthia, the sister of his great friend from college, Martin, in 1965 and set up house just down from the dock and fishmeal factory in Grimsby. They have witnessed a massive change in the local fishing industry over the 40 years since the 1960s. In the old days girls gutted fish on the dock and odd bits and pieces they didn't want were sent down to Pyewipe to the fishmeal factory. Then Iceland fishing was banned and now huge vessels return from all over the world full of 'partially processed fish fingers'. The trade is huge, rarely is an actual fish seen, one even wonders if in some foreign waters there is a new breed of genetically modified fish swimming around called the 'battered finger fish'!

The story of David's adventures in Iran, Panama, the Arabian empty quarter and by the Dead Sea and the city of Amman in Jordan are recounted in his first book 'Gently thru' life' published in 2000. The expectation thereafter was for a quiet life based at the Old Vicarage in Uttoxeter, then almost refurbished, but this was not to be.

After a series of frightening but interesting jobs on various local water recovery plants (that's down the sewage works) he became responsible on site for the extensions to Melbourne Water Treatment works, the job taking three years to complete between 1994 and 1997; eventually providing clean water to a higher standard to over one million people living mainly in Leicestershire.

After which he was persuaded to go for election as a councillor in local government. After a lifetime spent in the commercial sector this certainly was a change. Then, whilst his back was turned, on to the position of mayor both of his local town of Uttoxeter and then as Mayor of the Borough of East Staffordshire. This could be described as extending right across the gamut of life's expectations between pulling the chain and wearing one.

During this time he attended, mostly with his wife Cynthia, more than 400 engagements. This proved to be an excellent platform from which to find out what actually was going on in both the Council and the voluntary sector around Burton and Uttoxeter so as to present this slightly humorous slant on all the major local events going on at this time.

DJW, 8 February 2007

Chapter 1

'RECOVERY WORK' BACK IN UK

"How do you tell clean water from raw sewage laddie?"

"Err, err well ..."

"Sewage comes at you laddie – you can't stop people especially first thing in the morning. It's like it's fired at you in a rush down that channel ... either you handle it or get out of the way!!"

Then with frightened voice, *"What about clean water?"*

"That comes out of a glass all civilized. So what else do we likely need if we're not going round like bloody natives having sex all round and carving each other up?"

"Err, errr"

*"You need to know to get rid of these 'ere parliamentary dictators and vote proper for local democracy, that's what we all want get in there – **sort it out laddie**."*

This discussion took place in the restroom of a sewage works in rural Derbyshire. We call it 'a sewage works' not its proper name 'recovery works' as 'sewage' sums it up with that smell we all recognize. These rest rooms are surprisingly cheerful places where hands do tend to be washed before munching sandwiches, and where above all they know this is where the buck stops, whether it be by means of the gulley sucker or nose down with the traditional shovel – they'll need to keep their sense of humour.

But this was now 1989 and nothing had basically changed for a hundred years in the sewage treatment business. Storms still overflowed treatment plants into water courses and the whole industry depended upon a few hundred key workers who were prepared to 'go in and dig it out' at health risk to themselves in an emergency.

In the years I had been overseas technology had come on apace. Programmable units had become more reliable and user-friendly making possible remotely operated units with one or two operators only on site. The plant could be operated effectively, efficiently and automatically making the best progress in sanitary ware since dear old Mr Crapper in Victorian times.

Then following up as mayor in two separate doses, some might say was equivalent to wearing instead of pulling a chain, events did become even more rewarding and fun ... but as you will see it did become a little over the top at times.

1

Back to UK with a splash … ugh! My big Misconception

In March 1989 the client in Jordan finally ran out of money and I was obliged to wind up our office in Amman. On the classic basis of 'the last man remember to turn off the lights,' I left the familiar office and tried to forget the most interesting job I'd ever had – the fun and the anxious moments on our new ring main around the city, the new reservoirs (now at last not leaking), the wells down by the Dead Sea, floating around there sometimes on our day off like so many Brits of old in the 1950s. In those days they were trying to help the Arabs in Transjordan as it was then, understandably not making much progress lazing around with a newspaper in one hand and balancing a G&T in the other; at least you couldn't do that in the average UK swimming pool … all behind me now. Driving along to fifth circle, turning left down the Airport Road, boarding Royal Jordanian, back to UK and likely down to earth with a crunch or possibly a splash. What now for the future?

On the plus side our work over the past five years refurbishing where we lived at the Old Vicarage in Uttoxeter (which also used to leak) was nearly complete and more important was to see more of Cynthia and the boys and to get the family together once more.

Yes, a super family, the house nearly complete, but no job. I worked for a British firm of consultants who had for years worked almost exclusively all over the world in the clean water and sewage industry. So far for me only clean water, but this was about to change.

The sewage industry is known more accurately as the water recovery industry to include everything domestic and chemical, liquid or sometimes solid, that is put down the drains. I was soon to learn that examination of the works inlet bar screens was both symptomatic of the more private parts of our way of life and a subject in itself. One indeed which never fails as a topic of conversation. Sewage is sewage however, we all recognise the smell and know to keep well away or we will catch something don't we?

These consultants had massive objectives, providing water supplies and domestic sewage plants for whole populations of people in the Middle East and elsewhere. Amazingly they had gone a long way in some areas in reaching these objectives as follows: after the basic uncivilised 'pot on the head stage,' very harsh indeed on the women and young girls, there was drilling of new wells, possibly provision of a small reservoir, then pumping piped water to each village as stage one. Water consumption increased by around seven times as the locals got themselves and their clothes much cleaner, then they were in need of stage two which was gravity sewers leading to treatment works. It was said that these improvements in hygiene saved more lives than the doctors. Of course we need both.

As always with such fine objectives greed, dictators and politics more than lack of finance put a complete stop to progress on these matters in certain areas. So regretfully the job still awaits, either to be done properly, or in some cases to allow proper repairs to be made, in many parts of Africa, the Middle East, and South America.

However my preference in those days was to keep away from political matters and to get on with the job, anyway I now wanted a job nearer home.

As I touched down at Heathrow airport (I think I must have been eating pies up there in the clouds) my clear view was that drinking tap water must be fine, it always had appeared to be so previously in the UK, surely a drink of tap could not be improved now, furthermore not one drop in our drains was left untreated so what was then left to be done?

The next seven years were spent confirming to myself, as improvements came so thick and fast; that these first clear impressions were truly and completely rubbish, and at the same time I was being dragged by peaceful but subtle underhand means into the dreaded world of local politics.

What was on offer in UK? Discussion with Consultant

'A common water supply is used for drinking water and for general wash down of everything including toilets. This common supply comes from wells and large river intakes depending upon availability, treatment is by ferric sulphate together with sand filtration, including helpful bacteria, and sterilising is based on chlorine with some smaller wells using ultra violet light. In general there are a multiplicity of recovery works mostly based on anaerobic then aerobic treatments only. There are a multiplicity of small plants in rural areas together with large city treatment plants.'

At the interview it all sounded so tedious and stupefying simple didn't it? One tended to snatch a quick glance up at the ceiling and wonder where it would all lead, I had not long to wait.

As I talked further with my consultant bosses, the job no-one really wanted (and the one clearly coming my way) was for a 'large screw' at a sewage works at Stourbridge south of Birmingham, the mind boggled.

Rather frightening, this apparently was a proper sewage works and a large one at that, and I suppose it would need a large screw as well I suspected, possibly with my help. I'd never been in one of these places, let alone as one might say, put up a screw in one. I mean people normally don't do they? I couldn't chicken out on this now, it might mean LMF for me (nasty RAF term for lack of moral fibre).

I didn't want to turn the job down because I didn't know how easy it would be to get another and it was with the old firm. Anyway I thought this kind of job can't last long and eventually something nicer might come along, so thinking of England, bowler hats and umbrellas, to hell with the consequences, I accepted.

Next better get down to basics, it couldn't be all that bad, people actually work in these places, bet they are nice guys mostly. (I had to be right at least once). I found out that the smell itself won't harm you, but I didn't fancy carrying it home and worse back into bed; on a more civilized note what happens when you reach the stage when all of a sudden during the first course dining with friends you wish you had changed and properly showered before dinner?

Also I was grimly warned that insects buzzing around the bug beds can carry nasty disease so you might need a mask. So what was a bug bed I wondered and do we have one at home? Again I did my homework and found these were those circular tanks full of stones sprayed on from the top by sparge pipes, not all that inspiring I must say.

Then I read up about the traditional danger with nearly all sewage works. This wasn't a danger as such but they needed to be situated at the bottom of the hill to let gravity do the work and nearby at the bottom of the hill invariably there was the local stream full of fisherman and the odd fish. If storm conditions were maintained, after a while, at any rate until the 1970's and possibly later, the intake works filled up and overflowed. Dark unmentionable liquids poured out from the overflow pipe, the outlet invariably directed being towards the stream, contaminated it and killed a few fish (because that's all there were to start with) and sent the fishermen scurrying somewhere else. Unfortunately when the storm passed and the situation got better the fish remained dead and that was that.

At that time with poor collection of data, sometimes unavoidable, sometimes deliberate and no real regulations no-one really knew what was happening at the early stages. It was left to Public Health Officers to pick up the causes when the situation became more serious and the people – including the fishermen – got sick.

Fortunately for all of us this matter has now been tightened up and regulated for a number of years in this country both by the NRA who do the inspections and by EU who publish the regulations. OK so I had the griff but just how long would I last?

Stourbridge sewage works even compared with some dubious overseas experiences appeared to me at the start as a kind of hell, but without the devil and his toasting fork – it was far too cold for that sort of thing. When I first nervously attended site and met the smell (as you do even in winter), what made

4

it worse was the surroundings, everything was so dark, drab and grey and what didn't come into this category one was better to ignore!

January out there was bitterly cold with global warming not invented and certainly not worried about. Would you believe the job as it turned out was most interesting. It consisted of installing and putting to work a large inclined screw pump with around 5M lift, I had never seen anything like it before. The installation, looking from the side, was triangular in concrete to support the machinery. The outer sides had been provided with an attractive textured surface by means of special shuttering. Quite incongruous, a bit like Lady Godiva in a bowl of muck you might say, but even in this place you need to start somewhere.

You might describe it as screwing around with Archimedes whilst the winter sun, an orange ball peering out through the haze, skimmed just over the bugbeds before setting if still visible behind a large concrete sludge tank. At least I could retreat back into my site cabin occasionally for a cup of tea and a warm. However as was often the case in these places, the lads on the job were generally very cheerful and positive at all times even when it neared the time to go home.

Eventually we connected up the large motors and the screw finally went round. The sewage ran up the screw just like we were taught in our history lessons at school, before gently slopping out at the top into the high channel.

Ureka! – sorry wrong story – after the usual final touches were complete and the screw was screwing nicely I was released (along with Margaret Thatcher who was obliged to give way to John Major at this time), my best reward being the privilege of attending my very last traffic jam at the M6/M5 junction as usual on the way home.

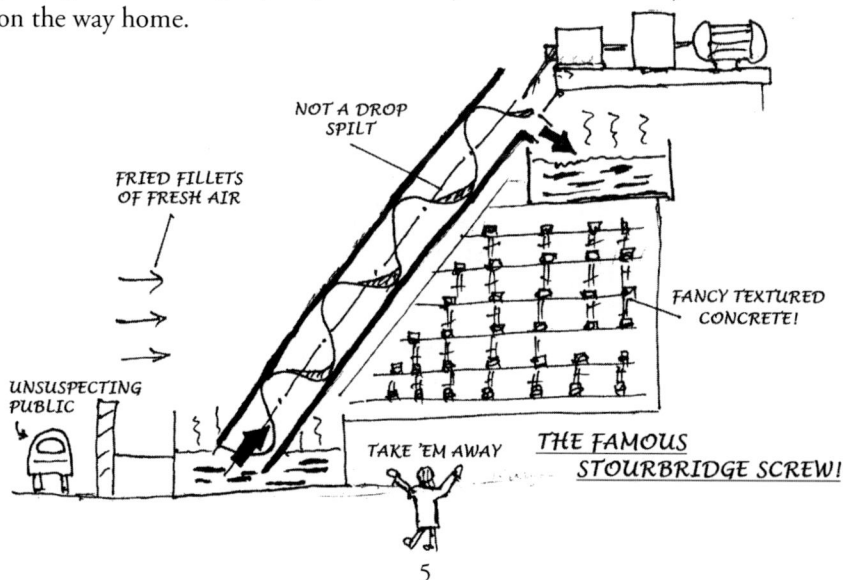

NOT A DROP SPILT

FRIED FILLETS OF FRESH AIR

FANCY TEXTURED CONCRETE!

UNSUSPECTING PUBLIC

TAKE 'EM AWAY

THE FAMOUS STOURBRIDGE SCREW!

Leek Recovery Works is in North Staffordshire. Leek is a town famous, in addition to being one of the highest towns in England, for its special soft water just right for its dye works, its chemical works and most especially for snow cancelling cricket matches – through the town runs the river Churnet.

This river was the subject of many complaints from fishermen and others convinced that the colour of their fish came from the colour of the river which in turn depended upon the shade of blue being used for the current run of jeans together with the tint of whatever else was in fashion at the time. They were right, the sewage discharge from domestic sources mixed with that from these works resulted in a special brew which the local recovery plant colourwise was unable to properly treat.

Accordingly the works were to be revamped at great cost to the taxpayer starting with new much improved biological and chemical treatments. Removal of final colour from the discharge was to be affected by a large ozone injection treatment system. This was part of our remit to see properly designed and installed. The plant represented an advance in technology. The local authority were rightly proud of what was being proposed.

We had no problem with all this but unknown to us the locals simply could not resist dribbling it out to the local press, unfortunately for us far too early and well before the plant was to be properly commissioned. Even the most common of common sense would dictate that these matters are best held very close to the chest until the river showed sparkling clean again.

The dye works management, being avid readers of the local press, had by now read all about it and the word had got properly around. They then, realising that no additional cost was involved, took the opportunity of flushing all available dye tank bottoms together with various colourful odds and sods down into the drains. This had resulted in a fairly spectacular range of colours in the effluent as we approached commissioning time. The fish I was told (without confirmation) looked like Joseph's coat of many colours. We remained confident however that even this amount of colour could be adequately removed by the equipment installed.

The colour removal plant was special as it included an ozone generating plant. This worked, just as we read about at school, by passing air through a high-voltage electric discharge then dissolving the gas in water which is connected by pipework to an injection system. This was sprayed into the flow stream sewage outlet through spray nozzles (for some reason called flying saucers, aptly named as it turned out) contained in a large reinforced concrete tank around 100M long. A number of baffles were fitted in the tank to divide

6

up the flow to make sure all the flow would be properly treated.

The first part of the commissioning went well. The ozone generating plant was tested, and the flow through the tank when previously tested separately, initially looked satisfactory.

It was at points such as this where engineering becomes a fascinating profession; however when you're in the thick of it (and there was certainly enough of this around) you rather wish you worked at the checkout at Tesco's.

I was looking after a small team including a young completely innocent student whose name was Gareth. His job was to collect samples from various sections of the tank for colour testing in the colorimeter, these results could then be assessed against required plant performance.

We then turned on the pumps, quickly scanned plant conditions for obvious faults before giving the plant a little time to settle down.

Gareth was a cheerful fellow I remember him well, he used to wear a Swansea rugby shirt being a keen supporter. He did have a certain casual attitude common to all students in whatever they were doing at the time. In this case taking samples of colour at the entry and exit of the ozone plant. Little did we know that any frustration on our part at this time would just add to our embarrassment later. He duly returned with the samples which he tested through the instrument and rather sheepishly announced that the plant appeared to be putting colour in rather than removing it!

This didn't worry me greatly at this stage, I just asked him to check more carefully just where he was taking the samples from and to repeat the tests, unfortunately one or two members of the team could not resist making funny remarks which we much regretted later. He duly returned, repeated the tests and once again, sure enough, there was more colour in the tank outlet stream than the inlet.

I was then asked directly and politely by the local management what I would suggest we did about it (no swearing or gnashing of teeth as yet). Fortunately it was almost going home time so I tactfully suggested we might make some proposals in the morning when we knew more of what was going on. Of course there was then frantic activity to sort out the cause. This only became clear when we examined the treatment tank. I suppose we were relieved in some ways to find it was a problem of materials. The flying saucers, not being properly resistant to ozone which is very corrosive, had chosen to become detached and were lying in a pile at the bottom of the tank. During the trial the flow was effectively not being treated at all. Those dramatic effects were due to a slight reduction in colour at the inlet during commissioning. Hence the £multi million plant appeared to be adding not taking out colour!

The lesson here is never advertise your success until it actually happens because it may not. You will be glad to know that after some delay to change materials the plant at last came properly on stream but the Wardles dye works did not. It was knocked down in favour of a housing estate.

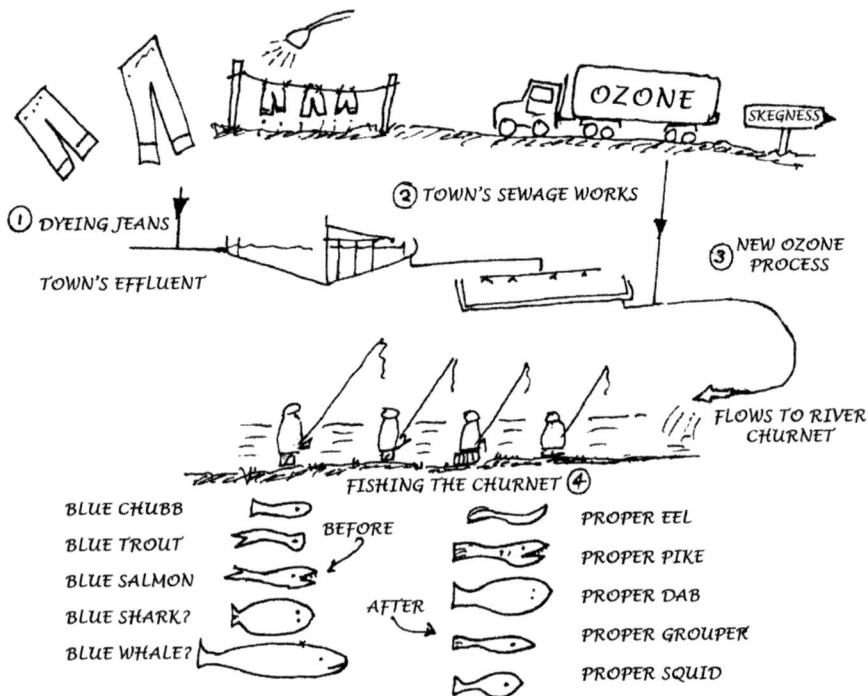

① DYEING JEANS

② TOWN'S SEWAGE WORKS

OZONE

SKEGNESS

TOWN'S EFFLUENT

③ NEW OZONE PROCESS

FLOWS TO RIVER CHURNET

FISHING THE CHURNET ④

BLUE CHUBB
BLUE TROUT
BLUE SALMON
BLUE SHARK?
BLUE WHALE?

BEFORE

AFTER

PROPER EEL
PROPER PIKE
PROPER DAB
PROPER GROUPER
PROPER SQUID

Rumblings of something big

As you can gather from my misapprehensions listed earlier, I had no idea of the *Rumblings of something big* about to happen to the water industry in the UK. I little realised that soon a series of golden eggs were to be provided. These would allow really significant improvements and savings to be made to the great advantage of all concerned and this meant lots of work for the future.

The cynical might conclude that all this was thanks to a combination of UK political dogma, sheer luck, and the import of the latest technology from silicon valley in the US. There is certainly something in this. In fact can you believe when all this started to happen, users were not treated as customers, just those who turned on the taps and caused a nuisance by all using the toilets at the same time in the morning. The kind of impudence which put you down in some peoples' eyes as old fashioned British; change was certainly needed.

We had lagged much behind many countries of Europe in the quality of our drinking water supplies because they now drank mainly bottled water and wine which eased their problem. We needed to treat all water supplies to drinking water standards. Thanks to our famous arrogance based I suppose on embarrassing tummy problems on the coach back from school trips to France, in no way were we as a nation prepared to admit to this in any way shape or form.

So what were these golden eggs now being presented to us on a plate, were they for frying or perhaps gently boiling?

The first egg was about organisation. From what I could see without any serious future planning, but quite a bit to do with politics, the industry had been privatised. This however was a fine move whether planned or not. It had both the effect of releasing finance to get on with things and more importantly control of finance was put in the hands of the 'sort it properly and quickly' set. Just what was wanted.

The second egg was a creeping one. Information Technology had improved over the past 10 years or so to the extent where it had been both abbreviated to IT and had made it possible to provide reliable signals to central control rooms showing exactly what was going on at the many and various outside sites. Vital information on levels, flows, plant breakdowns and water quality was now becoming available in central control rooms. One could only note with respect that this would have saved many lives if it had been available down the East Coast in 1952.

At the same time however, we could see typically that it was 'no change' on the old methods of doing the job. You could see on most roads 'team water' consisting of a van, two men, a maintenance schedule with some ticks on it, and some odd spares; all off to some obscure pumping station, dozing off with no real advice available nor communication with base. Yet this was about to change, it was the men themselves who caused it, and thus presented the industry with the second golden egg.

Yet these guys were the lucky few with secure jobs in very uncertain times whilst many were being laid off in other industries, furthermore they were getting away with the old inefficient ways of doing the job. Status quo prevailed – that is until some key maintenance workers thought to flex their muscles at the expense of the public and so went on strike.

Disappointingly for them, the country then did not immediately grind to a halt as expected. Water supplies amazingly remained largely intact for the period of the strike with some help from local management. This time lag thus led to the clear possibility that nearly all short-term maintenance could be triggered from telemetry. Management then with proper notice of trouble found their teams liked attending breakdowns well prepared and ready to get on with the job. Far better than cruising around bored looking for a bit of action to boil up, unable to act until it until it became really urgent.

Thirdly as if this were not enough, programmable computers (again abbreviated to PC's) became truly the third golden egg. These logic drives had been on the whole unreliable mostly due to their lack of user friendliness when I had left the UK five years earlier. Now they were available and could be programmed much more easily to control operations. For instance under storm conditions to sequence valves diverting flow to special tanks, to prevent overflow into water courses and later to operate more sophisticated systems, but to get them going we needed programmers.

To be a programmer you required fair intelligence, zero dress sense, a funny haircut, to be under 30 years of age, to be able to swing on a greasy swivel chair with bottom tightly compressed inside black almost threadbare jeans, to know about nothing except computers (but we did allow sex off the premises). Also on the plus side they were mostly also good fun to be with and had the ability, not possible before, to make adjustments based on verbal instructions 'whilst on line and running.' Maybe by now some have passed the age of 40, started wearing ties, being boring and driving street cred' cars – more the pitier I say!

Furthermore PC's are impervious to smell and clearly cannot see or react to even the most disgusting, horrible events occurring in close proximity. They just need a cosy waterproof box possibly slightly warmed to prevent condensation in the winter in order to perform a great control and monitoring job – out of sight, out of mind month after month year after year.

Unfortunately they won't yet do the washing up properly but this is being looked into.

Could there possibly be another egg, surely we now have a nest-full but no, there is just one more. I've mentioned smell before but if you lived say out in the sticks near a sewage pumping station the effect was like this. When the level in the tank was low the pumps stopped, the level rose and after a while the pumps started again and so on. The level went up and down and made a kind of 'smell pump' with smell coming out of the vent whenever the level rose. The fourth egg was the inverter which allowed through electronics the pump speed to change and these levels to remain much more constant, clever yes?

Whilst all this was happening things were beginning to slot in nicely on the home front. Where we lived at the Old Vicarage, restoration was now almost complete and, as people moved in to the new offices when they became available, this part of the house became full of friendly faces. The years of 'rotting silence with roof tiles falling like dandruff,' at last came to an end.

As a final splendid effort Billy's dad had remarkably removed no less than 100 tonnes of rubble in a wheelbarrow running on a plank through the window in the cellars. How do these old codgers do it? This raised the ceiling height in the cellars which enabled us to refurbish those as well. Only after certain bumping of heads did we realise that people grow taller these days than they used to 300 years ago.

To top it all we had the first wedding party with a marquee and the house full of people. The whole atmosphere of the place somehow reflected how things used to be in the old days, we hoped they would stay that way in the future.

Mind you I recall later there was that time, after serving the wedding breakfast, at the dim end of the serving tent where no-one was supposed to see, when one end of the table collapsed with one couple firmly aboard, they didn't seem to mind … but one has to keep tabs on the action for damage control purposes.

Chapter 2

Pure Clean Water At Last

First a confession; we had no special magic. We were subject to nature's laws like everyone else. Not once was I, or any member of the team, able either accidentally, on purpose, by magic or other means supernatural, able to persuade the prescribed amount of water to run up hill unless it was properly pushed or sufficient to go downhill as an overflow or whatever if the system was not properly designed. Indeed we found the bigger the attempt the greater the embarrassment. Having got this over back to the job ...

Where to go or where to be sent?

I wondered, the water companies following privatisation were now accepting the new computer technology and taking huge savings by changing methods of work. This was based on making full use of information from the new control rooms, data supplied by the telemetry systems recently installed. For short term maintenance, so essential to keep water flowing, effort was directed towards known failed equipment rather than sticking rigidly to inspections based on prescribed maintenance schedules, this also had the spin-off of improved safety as jobs could be examined back in the shop and proper facilities provided. On the downside, in order to improve standards to those required by regulation, was the huge cost of refurbishment of the old works one of which was at Melbourne (near Derby not in Australia).

For the larger capital jobs speed and accuracy could be improved by the use of far quicker site surveying methods; it was now amazing what could be done in a single day by use of the new laser surveying gear linked to the new 'computer aided design' methods in the drawing office. (known despite the connotations as CAD). On site both technology and suitable 'running gear' was needed. What was once done by the old chainman (he used a chain one cricket pitch long for measuring distance) and surveyor in two weeks was now done by a guy carrying a staff in running vest, shorts and the latest cool Nike shoes, the other guy acting as 'whipper in' issuing strange commands whilst peering through a digital theodolite.

My preference was to be involved at Melbourne and I was pleased to accept the job of looking after the electrical and mechanical works and commissioning of the job which started early in 1993.

I must say I had never been involved in such a large project and was lucky to attend this vast construction site for three years from the first turning of the earth to the time water was turned on to around three quarters of a million people living in Leicester, Loughborough, Ashby and places adjacent.

The works throughput of course depended on demand. The main objective was better quality but we were talking about something in the region of 200,000,000 Litres/day – this quantity is difficult to visualise but just the think of it as flooding the A50 between Burton and Derby – a stretch of 11 miles – each day to a depth of 1.1m (just over 3.5 ft). For the more pedantic readers this assumes water doesn't run away downhill but sticks to the carriageway at equal depth ignoring ground contours but let's not get too complicated.

Briefly water was extracted from the River Dove near Eggington just off the A38; if you drive along there it is just behind a large poster saying 'Water for All.' Untreated water from the river is pumped first to the reservoirs at Staunton Harold and Foremark before being passed to the Melbourne Treatment Works which is near the reservoir at Staunton Harold.

The existing distribution system which was already in place was curious in that all the water was directed east of the works, but nothing whatsoever to the west side. Nothing for Burton on Trent, so we had no responsibility for those special waters and the traditional pint of Burton bitter. As they all know in Burton, for ale wells under the town are used; for lager, a mixture of well and town's water (in this case mainly from Lichfield) is best.

Then for the big question; surely with things now on a much larger scale (the final cost was just under £50m) fewer errors would be made, there possibly might be less cause for humour, but at least with more attention to planning all this unscheduled hyperactivity following a 'problem' would be reduced?

I should have known better; these days they call it 'risk analysis.' This means assessment of risks as they might be anticipated. However we engineers are human beings and we should do our best but what happens if you either run up against something unforeseen or (heaven forbid) you just make mistake? (known in the trade as a c****p).

So as they say in tennis as they approach the final: the incidence of unforced errors was no less but their size and significance was purportedly that much greater.

What I did find important was that, although it all seemed very serious, having good relations and keeping a sense of humour was no less vital than before in keeping everyone in general from going bananas.

Looking back and getting pompous as oldies do I still remain proud of what was done during this period by the whole team working together including client, contractor and consultant to improve the health of the community. Particularly as we did the job over a three years period without cutting off water supply from anybody – however we will admit to having been uncomfortably close at times!

However before this started there was time to do some 'denitrifying.'

Milton

Those of you who have young families will know Milton. This is still advertised for sterilising baby bottles and if you are even older, not to say ancient like me, what we used in the old days to add to provide that extra reassurance to ensure towelling nappies were OK before they went through another recycle.

Here nothing could be further from the truth. Milton in this context was a delightful hamlet not far from Repton in the countryside just off the River Trent. The scenery is something to die for, activities in the area should be restricted to serious fishing, possibly some painting and some gentle farming to keep the locals warm on cold mornings.

What were we doing in these idyllic surroundings you might say? It was due to a generally potable water supply running continuously to waste into the Trent. This, although of comparatively small throughput, could be useful at the nearby treatment works at Melbourne under certain conditions to balance supply and demand. Anyway no-one wants to see a water source like this going to waste.

Stourbridge treatment works and the other recovery plants being now well and truly forgotten, here amongst the birds and bees in the countryside, dealing with clean water and a very interesting project – what more could you want?

The idea was to utilise this as part of Melbourne Works water supply but it needed to be augmented by a local well further down the road. The only other problem was that nitrates were high and this was considered detrimental to water supplies, particularly to babies and small children.

An old treatment plant existed on the site consisting of two resin columns working on a flow/standby basis. It was our job to reinstate the old system and bring it forward as the first fully automatic computer (PC) controlled system in use by the water company at that time, new ground and all very exciting.

The resin used in the columns consisted of small beads around 3 mm diameter (enough to make a real mess on the floor if any escaped). The water flowed through one resin bed which required regenerating from time to time by means of a salt solution from a large tank at the back of the works. In the meantime the other column was put on stream.

The first bit of fun was sorting out the automatic control. This we did in hiding at the contractor's works near Birmingham. A board was rigged up with switches and coloured lights linked to the PC. We then simulated the operation of the plant by moving the switches and watching the lights which represented the various valves turning on and off. This we did a sufficient number of times until we were really confident in the software. I was thrilled to bits using this method which was the only one I could see might work, I must say in conjunction with a very co-operative contractor. It was a bit like going to work to just to play some kind of pleasant pastime like jigsaws which you tried again and again until you succeeded.

Later I learnt that this very method was used to sort out the PC control for those death defying rides at Alton Towers. This ensured that a parallel back up system with a suitable fast response became available in an emergency ensuring proper safety for the general public. Now of course this sort of thing is commonplace. Hopefully it is still fun.

Up the road there was this well at a place, aptly known as called Sandy Lands, which we needed running to augment the supply.

Next a bit about wells. They are truly fascinating things and so basic to our way of life. Without them much of the world's water supply could not be made available to us.

In the old days wells were hand dug and needed to be fairly large in diameter, stay over 1m, in order that a man with a spade could get in there both to dig the well and line it. This was usually done with brick or cut stone. This was primarily to stop it caving in but also to keep water from rushing in at too great an extent as he approached the water table. He also needed some more brickwork on the top of the well to prevent ingress of surface water, the major source of contamination. In this country wells are invariably in some kind of shelter to keep rainwater out. In the desert this is not the case, no rain so wells were capped with a plate only. This allowed camels the opportunity of drinking by turning on the tap on the sample point with their teeth just downstream of the well head. They then left their mark in the form of many small spheroids of camel dung around the place, just what you need near a drinking water supply. Amazing creatures, they can even smell water in an underground plastic pipe under the sand, dig down and tease open the pipe at ther joints which I then needed to tighten back before the sun rose too high in the morning.

The water was extracted by hand normally by women by means of jars which were then carried on the head sometimes for long distances to place of residence. However enough of this, back to Milton.

We have progressed since these days of the bucket and rope. Wells are drilled, for water are normally not more than 30m deep, with diameters generally not more than 0.3m. During the drilling of a well a casing is slid down the hole to prevent it caving in and to provide a series of slots ensuring that water is drawn only from the chosen aquifers at certain known depths.

Drilling means that the total depth of the well can safely be taken down well below normal water table. After pumping when the water is at rest, the level rises and then falls as the pump is switched on. The performance of a well is checked by means of a level measuring device, usually these days an ultrasonic instrument.

Water extraction is done by means of a pump of cylindrical form attached to the outlet pipe, which is made out of a series of sections screwed together of total length around 30M depending upon well depth.

Enough of these technical details down to the actual nitty-gritty! It was no coincidence this particular well site was known as Sandy Lands. Once the new well pump had been installed and everything connected up, done with some difficulty by a crane lifting sections of pipe one after the other, the moment of truth arrives when the pump is first started up. Under these conditions sand or loose particles are invariably sucked into the pump, the discharge for this reason is passed to drain. Not for nothing was it called Sandy Lands. There are two choices: either the pump with some minor scrunching and flickering of the amps gauge will start, or the quantity of sand will be too much and the pump will grind to a halt. Hopefully you have set the overloads correctly and the pump will cut out on its own accord rather than burn out the motor down at the bottom of the well. The only choice under these circumstances is to gently reverse the direction of the pump. Hopefully reverse running does not result in a pump screwing off the end of the pipe and dropping down the well; with luck the pump will start and move sufficient sand so later it runs properly in the right direction.

All the time the dread is that once again the pump will not start and you are left pulling the whole assembly out and starting again.

At this stage it is best to remember that dropping things down the well is not to be recommended as later when blocking becomes severe reducing the active depth of the well, the situation can only be investigated by means of a CCTV camera. When this is done those responsible for the various misdemeanours are exposed and admissions of guilt can only follow. – 'I never dropped that spanner etc.' Incidentally the only way to remove debris was by means of a special cruncher which after doing its work allows the larger bits to be removed. I always found wells quite fascinating.

There was another curiosity on this plant. From time to time it discharged a fairly harmless dilute salt solution to reactivate the resin. This went down a mysterious pipe, so one day I followed it to investigate. It ran down the road across a field then very discretely into the River Trent at a place so delightful you could imagine mole and ratty appearing with all the ambiance of 'The Wind in the Willows.' No problem here, but was there?

If you looked carefully on this bank nearby were a series of numbers. On careful inspection you could see they were used for very serious fishing competitions. I often wonder whether drawing number 29 next to the discharge pipe brought a catch of prime salt water cod or halibut, but what a complete joy for those who could to spend a day fishing, looking for a bite in the sunshine amongst the gently swaying trees, staring across to the bridge and out to the church spire beyond.

We eventually got the plant running which was then used by the client from time to time on an intermittent basis which with many stops and starts was always a disadvantage with something as complicated as this.

However there was more. It is true to say that this plant, situated as it was in a very remote country area, then had a success which was totally unexpected. This would you believe came from the police. Based on a tip off, they had suspected for some time a farmhouse just within sight of the plant was being used by a gang of drug dealers. With the client's permission they installed some high-powered telescopes and, after watching on a 24/7 basis through the windows in the control room, were able after a while both to catch these criminals and then put the blighters away for a good time in clink where they truly belonged.

Although I was able to attend this site from time to time during the construction of a nearby site at Melbourne I must say I was sorry to leave Milton; it was certainly number one from being both attractive and as an interesting challenge.

Back to Melbourne with a proper job

For this reason it was with a certain amount of trepidation that I first attended site at Melbourne. This time there was the Chief Resident Engineer to look after the civil side, and I would be spending around the year preparing for all the other bits and pieces to arrive to enable the plant to work. At which stage the civil boys would disappear and I would be on my own.

Although I had seen many civil works before, this time I was unprepared for the sheer volume of activity.

First in came the big machines to tear out the earth, these were shortly followed by columns of dirt trucks, all the same design, rapidly piling up huge mounds of spoil. These reminded me of the old sand dunes from my time in the desert, except they were cold and wet instead of baking hot and dry. As an aside – did you know if you ran down a sand dune it groans loudly as if you have punched it in the stomach?

Back on track to say the work carried on whatever the weather (they don't allow such things to stop them these days) and soon six huge tower cranes arrived. During the night and at weekends they left the jibs swaying in the wind like huge birds looking for something to eat but really it was to reduce the stress on these very tall structures.

After some base concrete was placed in the bottom of each hole there came tons and tons of reinforcing steel to be carefully placed and secured to be carefully measured and checked as exactly as per the drawings. For the larger water retaining structures you could hardly see through the reinforcement. We called these bird cages, but no time for thinking around about aviaries before in came the wooden shuttering together with columns of transits (known to the world as concrete-mixer lorries) and the final structures began to take shape.

We had of course to make sure there were enough holes in the concrete to carry all the many electric cables running in and out of the buildings. Boring holes in concrete later for this purpose is, as its name suggests, both boring and time-consuming as well as embarrassing for those in the know.

Whilst we were looking at the structures in came another phalanx of lorries this time bringing in the massive amount of interconnecting pipework required for the works. These pipes, which were unusually made of glass lined plastic (GRP), became our first problem. Whereas they were perfectly fit for purpose when consolidated in the ground and with the seals modified so as not to leak they were a considerable headache whilst getting to this stage.

A remarkable engineering solution in the end saved the day. Underground pipelines are first consolidated in the ground with a small amount of backfill before being subjected to rigorous pressure testing. If leaks are found above the specified rate then attention is required and this was the case here with one of the underground pipes which by then – to my great annoyance – was buried 6M underground. However as the pipe was large enough to crawl down it could be repaired from the inside by applying a special extra seal fitted across the joint between the lengths of pipe. This proved remarkably effective. The other problem with these pipes was that, being much lighter in weight than steel pipes, were much 'livelier' when pressure was applied. They needed to be securely tied down under all pressure conditions. However careful you were, after one or two doubtful happenings with certain members of the team pursued by bits of pipe, you at least made sure everyone had a clear retreat however safe it looked.

Not much humour in this but in the end the job was OK and there was always the bar afterwards. Interestingly the savings associated with the use of these pipes over conventional steel (which were considerable) just about paid for the remedial works. The seal design was later improved but unfortunately only in time for their next project.

At this stage the machinery began to arrive and the various process buildings began to take shape. The process remained basically conventional for such water treatment plants with a few differences. The first stage which was for the removal of the larger particles by means of ferric sulphate was achieved by dissolved air flotation. (DAF). Interesting this including a beach made in sloping concrete provided for removal of filtration debris from the water surface after flotation rather than by gravity. (no deck chairs, ice cream or sunglasses provided here)

This was followed by refurbishment of around 60 existing sand filters. This was a wise move by somebody in the design department. Sand does the filtering job by building up special bacteria which enable water to be filtered to a much greater extent than by straight physical particle filtration, backwashing with water was required after so many hours. (clever eh?)

These filters had old fashioned automatic valves but overall did not look too bad. However when we took them apart we found an absolute can of worms. Every valve leaked internally in a way you couldn't tell unless whole sections of the plant were shut down. When a backwash was called for, water was going to all parts except where it should be. This reminded me of that old boy at Ripley sewage works who asked me, *"What do you think it is like getting old?"*

"Cannot imagine," I replied.

He said after a pause, *"Laddie your dry parts get wet and your wet parts go dry."*

A huge granulated activated carbon plant (GRP) containing hundreds of tons of carbon was included to ensure a definite improvement on water quality. Unloading that quantity of carbon was a major operation both for us and also the suppliers who were limited in the amounts they could process.

I always believe in testing things on the basis of the worst thing that can happen, an incident on the site in the old days before telemetry illustrates this.

Weather conditions will search for a weakness in any system. For security, electricity to the works was and still is supplied by two high-voltage overhead lines. In addition the Electric Company for additional security had provided these from two separate sources. One snowy night when exceptional conditions combined a sharp frost with falling wet snow, this resulted in the snow settling on the overhead wires to the extent that eventually one wire was pulled down and the supply to the works was lost. Switchover then took place and power was restored to the works by the use of the second overhead line.

After a while this itself was pulled down for the same reason and on this dark and snowy night the works were left completely without power.

This was not itself disastrous as holding reservoirs could continue supplying water in the short term. However six miles away at Foremark reservoir, unmanned at the time, the off-take pumps continued running to supply water to the works which to all intents and purposes was dead.

At the main works the old primary treatment ponds at the top of the hill, receiving this flow, which could not be pumped away, promptly overflowed. What could described as a tidal wave (a minor tsunami you might say) then flowed down the hill and in through the front door and out the back of a row of quite innocent cottages at the bottom, one presumes they were asleep upstairs; no-one really was witness to the event were they? Fortunately no-one was hurt but all was not finished yet.

It was then necessary for the management to jump in the old Land Rover (not forgetting the keys to Foremark Pumping Station), then to drive the six miles and manually stop the pumps, all in a night's work. This fully illustrates how much things had improved over the past 10 years, and were about to do so again.

ELSIE - WAKE UP I CAN HEAR WATER RUNNING

DANNY - DO BE QUIET ... I'M STILL IN THE MIDDLE OF OUR BOAT TRIP OFF SCARBOROUGH

MELBOURNE WAY

With the shiny new plant and polished up computers we eventually arrived to the stage of testing safety overflows. On worst case testing, this particular one failed in the basic sense that it was diverting insufficient water to prevent the level in the basement just under the electric panels rising in a fairly alarming manner. Fortunately we were watching carefully and had plan B (Plan A was to panic, we hadn't dusted that one off for years) and with the aid of portable radios the flow was quickly stopped and the problem transferred from the immediate to the 'what on earth can we do next?'

This was solved by the fairly common principle for civil works – *bring in the Irish*! Using the thrust bore method (similar to that unsuccessfully used to provide a tunnel under the Thames in the 19th century) hydraulic jacks, a special pipe and a faceplate were rigged up and a set of amazing Irishman appeared with spades and a conveyor belt to remove the spoil from the pipe. In no time at all a bigger and better overflow pipe was thrust into the critical area which fortunately failed to run into any other adjacent underground pipes. (you could never be completely sure). However the solution proved 100% effective and further testing was successfully completed without the need for either wet feet, soaked computers or diving gear.

At the time sophisticated electronic devices called inverters were becoming commonly used to change pump motor speeds to better balance supply and demand. Inverters for our large duty pumps were bigger than the pumps themselves almost 3M high reaching almost to the ceiling. They worked by changing what was originally a perfectly smooth alternating-current supply as from the mains into a composite chopped up wave form of slightly differing frequency. This sure enough gave the necessary changes in speed which did the job.

However we had moved into one league too far in size and conventional items like transformers were not always happy with the amended chopped-up version of alternating-current supply and this resulted in some fairly dramatic effects on start up.

These primarily consisted of a fairly large bang, puffs of black smoke, nasty black residues inside the panels, and dramatic black marks on the ceiling marking the occasion and the whole situation became totally unacceptable.

Fortunately again no-one was hurt. To get round the problem the manufacturer was forced to furiously uprate components and run the motors only according to strict limits. At one stage the available pumps were reduced to only two out of seven. Everybody including the Water Company worked furiously for long hours trying to sort out the problem, their knowledge of where available water was in the overall system was a vital part of the temporary solution. The nasty part was that the effect of the changed electrical waveform at these power ratings was outside the scope of the theory then available. We were clearly in the wrong place at the wrong time.

However the key thing as I had learnt way back in the earlier days was to work together as a friendly team and do the best you can. We kept it like this and eventually the position eased.

It's funny looking back now how things can happen in practice. Just prior to this event it had been necessary to start up the plant just prior to the Christmas/ New Year holiday period. This was never a good idea and one which inevitably meant sorting a number of small faults somewhere or other and dragging people out of their beds just before the third verse of *auld lang syne*.

Understandably this programme did not find favour with the contractors. For one thing it involved large overtime payments. One boss was determined his men would not to be called out over this period unless he was contacted in person and with full details and I could tell it was doubtful if he would actually pick up the phone under these circumstances. The inevitable happened but at 11.45 on New Year's Eve when I was obliged to ring him at home. He was really for making himself scarce but assumed the call was to wish him a happy New Year – once of course contact had been made his team had to be out in no time at all to sort the problem out.

In the end a generally happy team working on the job were able to overcome unforeseen technical problems, in other words when the chips were down you found out who your friends really were.

Have you wondered about water shortages? In this country rivers, streams and most reservoirs, never completely dry up during the summer period, indeed water companies are obliged to release a certain flow downstream of dams into water courses (called compensation water) to prevent this happening. Levels fall and it is true to say that dry areas in streams and reservoirs do appear and well levels do fall. So we have hose pipe bans and urgent appeals to the public to reduce water consumption, usually from an official standing on a cracked dry part of the reservoir looking very serious, threatening standpipes and serious consequences if we don't all do our duty and reduce consumption. I have no objection at all to this approach except that reducing overall consumption also significantly reduces pumping costs both in the short term and, after it starts to rain, also in the long term. No bonus is ever offered to the consumer for reducing consumption, on the other hand the water companies are quite happy to privately pocket savings in pumping costs which amount to a proportion of the £1m/yr total electric cost (mostly for the big delivery pumps) typical for a large size treatment plant. From data readily available there could be derived an average savings per user on which a fair bonus could be based. Play fair please!

Nosing around and talking to people I soon found that counselling within the ward would be far more about talking and persuading than logic and the written word, although there still would be plenty of that! I had always strongly doubted the powers of persuasion unless they are backed up by some technical reason to indicate that least the argument was running in the correct direction. The main thing being that, if action was required, to do something about it but first there were the elections …

In addition I did believe I was too old to start as a councillor based on four-year separate sessions. I was persuaded this was not the case and in the end agreed to stand for Uttoxeter Town Council and for the East Staffs Borough Council. The idea was to feed local facts up from the Town to the Borough and at the Borough to be able to find out what was going on in planning, what our policies were, and other matters.

Chapter 3

NOSING AROUND, WONDERING ABOUT BEING A COUNCILLOR

The Decision

So things gradually sorted and the larger projects I was involved in became completed. Severn Trent were well able to take control of their new plant at Melbourne and after spending a further six months assisting with Derby water supplies, plus several extensions of time, I said 'thank you no more,' and made the decision to retire.

This led to the gentler world of local UK politics of which I knew absolutely nothing. I found we lived in Town ward Uttoxeter. I suppose my overall attitude was that it had the potential to be both extraordinary boring (same old hymn sheet over and over again) as well as to be quite unnecessarily complicated.

Canvassing – that's knocking on doors

Elections were imminent and it was necessary to go around canvassing, asking local people what their problem was and whether they were prepared to vote for me. (I soon found that one rarely gets the right answer to this one!) I had great difficulty in identifying myself with National parties as they fitted in with local politics but the Conservatives seem to have a more friendly relaxed attitude and in any case the Labour Party didn't ask me!

Yes canvassing is slightly frightening at first and it is better to go around with someone who knows the ropes although everyone ends up with their own particular style.

The one problem we never cracked was that of the ordinary common or garden domestic dog. You may visit 40 or more houses to lull you into a sense of security, in the meantime you forget all about dogs, only the postman knows where caution is required, but you don't.

Of course the electors feed (and sometimes overfeed) their dogs and this forms a special bond particularly for lonely people. A super friendly bond in which potential councillors are definitely not included. In dog's eyes councillors are a cross between something to just nip at or something to seriously get your teeth into.

No matter the size of the dog each has its own technique. There is a terrier quietly sitting on the back of the settee in the bay window. If you are just delivering literature you know you have around ten seconds. This is to get your fingers through the letterbox, drop the letter, and withdraw your hand – before the dog drops down from the settee, swerves to the left like Barry John down the hallway with the speed of light and launches seeking the last two fingers of your hand before slamming into the door with a sound like thunder.

At the other end of the scale there are the huge dogs linking as they often can do with quite elderly old ladies who shout their warning, coming round the side on the house unnoticed, with the large animal already in the pounce position having all four paws off the ground driving into your stomach like Will Carling. In response to your question, 'is that a Rottweiller?' its praises are fully described whilst you look around the side of their house frantically for possible means of escape.

The other bit of fun it is that row of terraced houses where you politely knock on the first door and after a reasonable time without response move onto

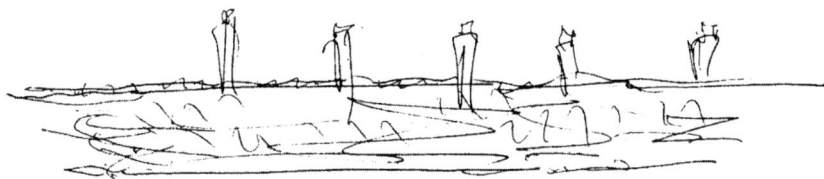

3 AT A TIME!

the second and then, again with no response, the third. At which time all three doors open simultaneously exactly on cue you're left with three constituents or all thinking this man is pretending to be busy without time to talk to us separately.

About this time I did however get a comforting feeling that local people in Uttoxeter were largely straightforward, unpompous and had a sense of humour which I very much liked. They called a spade a spade when necessary and if they talked too much it meant they voted for the other side. Despite all the rivalry that clearly went on between the two towns, Uxonians were really much like Burtonians whom I knew better having worked there 10 years previously.

One slightly scary feeling was that should I be elected as a councillor you looked after some 2000 people – it was hoped they all didn't write or come knocking on the same day!

Polling Day and what comes after!

At last the great day came, canvassing was over and our team in Uttoxeter increased by around eight temporary helpers who had come to assist with all the exciting things that go on during election day, all of which of course remain completely unknown to the great mass of people who are obliged go out to do a normal day's work.

Voter numbers remain small for Local Elections averaging only around 25%. Although this is disappointing it means that efforts from the local team can make a difference. For General Elections the figure usually rises to over 50% which, added to a bigger electorate, does tend to give you a little more confidence in the result.

A steady stream of the population then trudge into the polling booths throughout the day. When they close, the council officers heave a sigh of relief but only temporarily as the next thing is to send the boxes away for the count.

Election day can have its amusing side. It has been traditional for political parties to take old people, who have no transport, in to the polling stations to vote. This can be fun in itself as of course you never know which way the crafty old lady or gentleman will vote. As part of our democratic system if the person is disabled you are allowed to offer assistance out of your car and even as far as into the polling station and up to the booth (maybe with the assistance of a council helper to see fair play) but of course it is a criminal offence to put the pencil in their hand or say anything at this stage. Thereafter of course you are reasonably obliged (whichever way you think they voted) to offer assistance to them to return safely back to their home.

Even the best laid plans can go wrong however. I remember once contacting an old people's home in the country and arranging for taking a car full of old people determined to vote. Having happily filled my car with loyal supporters (or so I thought) they advised that not only were they not voting in my ward i.e. not for me, but their polling station was at Bramshall around 5 miles further down the road. I was therefore obliged to spend what seemed to be nearly all morning travelling out to Bramshall, watching whilst they slowly cast their votes presumably in favour someone of unknown, and after a good old chatter amongst themselves, allowing me to return them back.

However on these occasions I was often touched by the determination of these people to exercise their right to vote at a time when only around 25% bothered. Things have recently changed however and postal votes have been made available to all who want them. This has increased turnout by around 10% but does represent a large extra effort by council staff in processing all the paper-work. Before you say 'so what' please remember who foots the bill, you do.

Then came the excitement of the count. The first was held in Uttoxeter. I went to see votes counted and was grateful to win a Town Ward seat for the 'cauldron' which was Uttoxeter Town Council. There is something traditional and terribly basic about tipping out the boxes in front of the counters who are themselves scrutinised by someone sitting across the table, putting them into piles of say 100, then in piles for each candidate. When each candidate gets so many they are check-counted in a machine, then put in piles in a box at the end. By counting these piles you can see how you are doing. Then the following day in exactly the same way I was again successful at the more civilized and straight thinking Borough Council alongside my oppo. also called David (we later sometimes got mixed up, mainly to his advantage), for Town Ward Uttoxeter, and there we stuck for the next seven years!

So I was now a councillor. What had I done to deserve this? On the other hand did these people realise who they had voted in I wondered, we would see. Borough Councillors were paid a small sum (which came as pleasant surprise) and were able to sit on some interesting (hopefully non-political) panels like Planning and Licensing. If their party was in control they might make a contribution towards the policy of their party, or criticising the others if they were in opposition.

This number of postal votes has also finally finished the old process of 'telling.' Traditionally this meant a group of dedicated party workers usually supplied with a table and chairs sitting by the entrance noting down who had voted and advising their party office accordingly. If they did not know the person concerned they would ask them their electoral number. If they replied (and this could give the average busy person in a hurry the chance to be abusive) they could look up their name from the number on the electoral role and check if they had previously indicated their support. Those who had not been counted by the afternoon were reminded by telephone.

You prepared yourself to receive the flood of letters which now were directed at you on a regular daily basis. The awkward and interesting ones were always handwritten which meant from a constituent with a point to make. You then rang up the person and went round for a friendly chat. This could lead to anything but was essential in getting the feedback of what was actually happening, for instance that outbreak of squirrels.

The council had kindly agreed to remove the outbreak and got rid of a number of squirrels after two vigorous old ladies had complained. They had refered to them understandably as tree rats whilst watching them munching their way through their well-tended lettuce seedlings. The war continued whilst in the meantime on the other side of the side of the fence a family of 'nature lovers' had succeeded in encouraging them to build a fine nest in which they were feeding and breeding apparently without interference. The moral here is to think of the consequences before entering into agreements on behalf of the Local Authority but more than that – beware of old ladies, they have been around for a long time and may know what they are doing.

In practice thank goodness I didn't get too many of those hand-written letters from constituents. The reason for this was that problems tended to be common amongst the sections of the community. These could be handled in one shot, the question nearly always was how to get action, if that was wanted, without too much delay. However once or twice we were faced rightly or wrongly with renta-crowd!

With the rise in technology improvements have been possible and now laptop computers have been made available to all. The cynical would say that time spent previously wading through loads of paperwork is now spent trying to avoid reading the latest versions of the numerous viagra adverts which creep through into the council website and which no-one seems to know how to completely eradicate. So much for 'fire walls' and all the rest of the jargon.

Chapter 4

THE DIZZY HEIGHTS AS MAYOR OF UTTOXETER

The Bun Fight

I must say I never once gave a thought to becoming mayor of anything. In Uttoxeter our party had gained a knife-edged control after main election results which had gone like this. The two main parties were equally represented including one independent who in those days voted for the other side. However in local government the mayor has a second casting vote which had enabled us to claim control. (How this fits in with democracy I will never know.)

Now I had been a councillor for only two years and after this time I was being asked by our team to be Deputy Mayor of Uttoxeter. There was naturally a set procedure to go through before this goal could be reached. First I had to be elected as Deputy Mayor at the Town Council at a rather aggressive meeting. If successful I would be mayor the following year, which was really quite a sensible arrangement. Before the meeting I had troubled to establish that I could vote for myself. Although this went very much against the grain it was a good move, everything being so political – although it is well known that the office itself is supposed to be non-political! Anyway without my own vote the office would have gone to someone else and so despite the business of demanding a named vote with notes on scraps of paper counted in secret and witnessed in the clerk's office, it was my lucky day and I was voted in and Cynthia my wife later agreed to serve as consort. I did wonder to myself if this was really the way to behave.

I passed time as Deputy Mayor quite peacefully after that initial rumpus and one year later became mayor. I had now changed the sharp smell of the sewage works into the riper more distinctive odour of the cattle and sheep pens coming straight through the Town Clerk's window from the old cattle market, in those days situated directly outside the back of the Town Hall; a reminder of old times as you might say.

After the mayoral service, a year of office commenced. We were pleased to attend the various civic engagements which were presented at an agreeable pace, around two per week.

In Uttoxeter there are around 15,000 people which is just about the right size so you can with a bit of effort find out more or less what is going on by listening to and enjoying the friendliness of the many locals you meet. Not forgetting that this was the exciting time when the town was starting to 'wake up to catch up' at the very start of work towards the masterplan for the town. We were looking, with the help of the Borough Council, at what was going on elsewhere and also combining to choose a consultant to prepare the plan. In addition we needed to play our part in the Queen's Jubilee celebrations.

So how to record all these events in detail? First there are a selection of those interesting and amusing main events that made up the year. Then under the heading 'where were you in 2002/3?' providing details from information noted at the time telling us:

> Some useful advice for everyone
> What were people up to in the town?
> What developments were going on?
> What events were being organised?
> What help was the Town receiving?

The famous re-lighting of the War Memorial

After much effort in the town the war memorial was once more flood-lit at last. The lights were provided by the council but clearly would not have appeared at all were it not for Frank Slater – intrepid local undertaker, church clock winder, octogenarian, and member of choir going back to 1938.

When all had been prepared for the switch-on, Frank arranged for an interview by Radio Derby for publicity purposes and kindly asked if I could be there to support him. The interview took place in the pouring rain in the covered entrance to the Advertiser office in full view of the memorial. Radio Derby sent a very attractive Asian lady for the purpose. Frank was as ever looking trim and fit despite his years and the good lady took full advantage of this refering to his good health despite his age and confirming whether or not he was around when the memorial was first given to the town. Yes, he was a young lad at the time, then how remarkable that he had been able to ascend the church tower stairs to wind the clock for all these years and so on, the compliments flowed. I could see Frank was much enjoying this. However I considered the treatment to be well deserved so I was pleased to say silent in the background whilst Frank chest-out seemed to grow a couple of inches. After a while she then turned to me, introduced me as the mayor and said on air – I believe the memorial was originally provided with lighting and why was this taken down? I had no difficulty in explaining that this was part of the blackout at the beginning of the war in 1939. The lights were switched off as the first bomber came over. She then asked (I admit as tactfully as she could) if it really took 62 years for the council to take action on these matters!

So after all these years in darkness an appropriate switch-on ceremony was organised in the presence of the Staffordshire Regiment. This included their dog handler in his splendid uniform and of course the regimental dog in his splendid embroidered coat which included his present rank, which if I remember was corporal, plus of course a squad of men. The organisation to provide this was wonderful – a quick phone call – do you want the squad? The dog? The handler? was all that was needed to provide the necessary, I wish everyone was like this but I suppose the regiment needed all the recruits it could find at this time. As usual the local police kindly co-operated providing their specials to provide the necessary traffic security.

I duly went (draft speech in pocket) 'fully' prepared for the occasion except with no knowledge of the name of the dog. I approached the dog handler before the ceremony and he told me. In classic style I wrote this on a piece of paper which promptly did a disappearing act. When it came to deliver a short but well deserved thank you speech I came to the name of the dog – there was a short silence and a member of the squad in order to help whispered 'Winston 3.' I took his advice but on the way back was sure that I had made a mistake. So several beers later including some apology (some would say grovelling) to redress the situation only to find after all 'Winston 3' was his nickname the real name being 'Watchman 3.'

As an aside I have never owned a dog as a pet but clearly they can be superb companions for lonely people. Amongst these are also rescue dogs, who are rescued from unsuitable owners or from owners who have even left dogs to care of themselves. As part of this we were very pleased to support training facilities for dog owners, on the lighter side remembering on one occasion having a close call with a sheepdog who presented not only a large cheque for charity but a close call with some rather sharp canine teeth.

So when the time came during the ceremony the electrician surreptitiously opened the lower cover on an adjacent streetlight fiddled the timer and ever since the war memorial each night has been was well and truly lit.

The town's millennium monument

I suppose the most remarkable achievement the Town Council made during my first years as a councillor was sorting out a special millennium monument of which we could all be proud.

Of course the council consisted of a small number of people not all of whom were necessarily in favour of such things. In this case what happened was for a committee to be formed with members from both inside and outside of Council. If that group produced, with the assent of Council, something of quality then it would both follow the wishes of some people and also to make a pointer towards what might be of real benefit to the town. It was all a matter of principle and publicity and to hope that a fairly large section of people would accept it when the job was finished, not forgetting that there were those, including some on the Council, who would object to everything at this stage whatever was being proposed.

To add to this in the beginning we had neither the money nor the expertise in any department to produce something which might be special, some small donation was given by the Council plus some more from the general public which was gratefully accepted but not nearly enough. Then added to the pot was the uncertainty due to the recent change in the political leadership on the Council but fortunately it was our side who had won.

Then quite remarkably in view of all this the principle to go ahead was agreed. The team were to report back on a design prepared by the local company in Marchington (Hayes Industries) and some very good advice was obtained from our friends at JCB.

If the monument was to celebrate the millennium (2000 years since the birth of Christ) it clearly had to include time as the theme and some kind of sundial would be appropriate commemorating the first successful ways of measuring time. A suitable position for the monument was likely to be in the Market Square opposite Ye Olde Talbot inn.

A conventional sundial would be somewhat inappropriate as the gnomon (the pointer which shows a shadow on a dial indicating time, directed towards the North Star) would form a sharp upward facing object. This it was feared would be a danger to those exiting the pub on a warm evening for some fresh air not wanting to accidentally sit down for a rest on a sharp spike.

This time we were pleased to receive the kind assistance of a member of the British sundial Society who advised us that an armillary scale might be more appropriate. I must confess this suggestion went somewhat above our heads but he explained that with this design the shadow from the gnomon passes along a ground graduated inside scale and the danger from an upward spike was removed.

The next idea adopted by the panel was to use information available on the Internet from the National Observatory to establish the position of the planets as they were on the first of January in the year 2000. As the planets proceed round the sun in approximately the same plane their position could be represented two dimensionally on the top face of the monument. The planets could be represented by the different shades of granite most exactly copying the colours of the planets as seen from space.

The next idea, and we seemed to be full of ideas, was for a circular structure in stone 2M in diameter, each 1 mm of diameter equivalent to a year since the birth of Christ.

Then I rushed home and dug up some mathematics I had not wrestled with for around 30 years. First assuming an outside diameter of 2 metres, a suitable logarithmic scale was required for representing the distance between the planets on the top of the monument. The relative angles between the planets were available from the information supplied by the Royal Observatory so these could be incorporated also. As for the diameter of the planets, because of the huge discrepancy between the diameters of the planets and their distances apart, a separate logarithmic scale was required. The golden ball in the centre represented the Sun and a similar scale was used for this. The bronze casting into which the planets were fixed was deliberately cast rough to represent the darkness and uncertainty of space.

Following all these technical details, it was decided that we should commemorate on the monument local organisations and any special Uxonians who had made contributions in the past to the town and elsewhere.

Obtaining an agreement to this was difficult. We sent an open letter in the press for local organisations to come forward quickly if they wished to be mentioned on the monument, with instructions to respond well before stone chipping had started. In the end by a mixture of persuasion and downright insistence we managed to obtain a list of organisations with the general acceptance of all.

In a moment of fun (or maybe it wasn't) someone suggested that we include Bartley Gorman our famous gypsy boxer from Uttoxeter who was for some time world bare-knuckle champion in this now officially outlawed sport.

We were then supplied with a description of him and his achievements. Incredibly this proved to be the only text out of 16 submitted which was without some kind of error or spelling mistake. We were very conscious that it was not appropriate to include mistakes in the lettering on the monument designed to remain for a number of years so it had to be right. However after considerable effort from a number of people, no less than 60 errors were found in the wording of the 16 plaques. Again we were blessed with the solution, to ask for advice from Thomas Alleynes English department. They politely advised us of a further five errors.

Then there was some more fun for those concerned following the decision to incorporate a time capsule in the monument including the youngest and the oldest persons in Uttoxeter living on the first of January year 2000. Strangely we found two grand old ladies born on the same date, both almost 100 years old, to fill the role of the oldest. The youngest was more difficult to find as we had not thought of the rules as regards where births should take place. However we eventually overcame this, sorted out the rules and a little baby boy was chosen.

We then arranged with Highfield Nursing Home, where the two old ladies lived, to admit around 80 people to witness the two old ladies inserting certain notable town documents into the time capsule for later insertion into the monument by special means.

In order to achieve this it was necessary for me to persuade the matron to open the windows to reduce the temperature in the room to suitable levels to prevent distress to the attendees. This done all went well and now it was up to our famous stonemason to complete the work and transport the monument in pieces on to its final site.

Here it must be recorded that the stonemason made a remarkable job of finishing off the chamfered sides of the monument. This he did by chipping away by hand with considerable skill which I found amazing. Having transported the stonework to Uttoxeter it was necessary to lift the completed monument by means of a crane, then finally to settle it horizontal with the gnomon pointing at the correct north-south direction towards the North Star. Here again we ran into some trouble when we found local weathervanes in the market place pointing in all directions except north. Eventually we used a map, a compass, and the theodalite to get the positioning right. At last the monument was positioned and complete.

It was then left for the kind attention of the Earl of Shrewsbury to come for the official opening which included something we devised in conjunction with JCB's demonstration department. The Earl officially pulled a lever in one of their front loaders, the bucket was attached to a number of flags covering the monument which was dramatically unveiled for the pleasure of the people of the town and for all to see.

I must say my biggest dread at that time and since has been to receive a polite question (especially asked by a young person from the local school indicating an error in the mathematics and the need for some embarrassing stone chipping. You'll be pleased to know that up to now this is not yet happened but I suppose the jury is still out.

Children and ice cream cornets

Children are of course great levellers. Any attempt to pull wool over anyone's eyes, whether or not you were wearing that mayoral chain, is fraught with risk and possibly even danger, but more than likely to your ego.

I recall once in Uttoxeter supporting a new children's play park down Howett Crescent, a rather poor area and just where we needed something extra to amuse the very young ones. A very successful afternoon was had by all except my brush with the ice cream stand. The kind lady insisted on giving the Mayor two delicious ice cream cornets. These were fine but of course talking to people predominates and I had little time to give them each a good lick.

The inevitable happened, not noticing that each cornet had a hole in the bottom I had them both in one hand when both sides melted at once and jointly squirted straight down the front of my trousers right there into dangerous areas! In this case you find out who your friends are and where a discreet cloth and a bucket of water can be found. This being the only crisis I was pleased to go round all the stalls and afterwards having another appointment said cheerio to the organisers and wandered across out toward the car.

I noticed I was being followed by a young girl of about 10 or so I suppose who obviously had something pressing on her mind. She waited until I reached the car, there was a silence for a few seconds and she said, *'where's your limmo?'* I said something about saving the grown ups money on their tax bills and so on and she seemed satisfied. However every time later as Borough Mayor in the chauffeur car I looked anxiously out when we were in the area but fortunately she never appeared.

Who is or was Churchill?

During the run-up to summer exams at Thomas Alleynes School in Uttoxeter when many students had completed their exams I was very pleased to be asked to take a lesson on Civic Responsibilities. On arrival I found that this needed doing three or four times over (there were multiple streams) but thankfully a teacher would attend each session to ensure fair play. I explained something about civic responsibilities and how they had developed over the years and something on the sacrifices made in the past to achieve a democratic system we all enjoy in the present.

This however was not without humour and I arranged to ask each class a few of the same questions, not too difficult. One was 'who was Churchill?' The response from each class was good being something like 'famous World War II military leader' but one boy responded by saying – with or without tongue in cheek – 'a famous dog.' Whereas I was thinking of some kind of British Bulldog the rest of the class were on the ball with the cost of house insurance

Chapter 5

UTTOXETER – WHERE WERE WE IN 2002/3?

There is no doubt that our mayoral year 2002/3 saw the start of a seed change for the town. As we were given the opportunity of meeting many of those involved we were possibly in the best position to record at this interesting time exactly what was going on under four main headings:

People
Of course it is the people who make the town. So just what were their successes and failures at this time compared with the present day? In general what was their sense of humour really like?

Then what about that select group of people who both have the opportunity, and then take it, to work for the community in various ways as volunteers outside the demands of work and family? Is TV together with the many new attractions available whittling down even this small number? (I would estimate around 120 out of 12,000 people at this time fell into this category.)

Developments
Just what progress has been made since those first thoughts on town development: of a master plan for the town, a pedestrianised High Street, closing certain smoky old pubs, the horror (quite unfounded I believe) of a Weatherspoon's in the town, planning permission for flats within walking distance of the shops on the high street, developments on both sides of town Meadows Way, further improvements to Pennycroft Park and possible dry-play pitches at Thomas Alleyne's School?

Local Events
How do we stand on local events? Apart from Jubilee year which was special at this time, are present activities tailing off or increasing and since this time?

Help from outside
Local Authorities and local developers had a large input in changes made since 2002/3. Residents were in favour of change once they could see it was generally being made for the good of the town but how does this compare with the situation now?

These are interesting questions. In order you might suggest answers let us remind ourselves just what was happening under these headings in that period between September 2002 and May 2003, based on accounts made at the time.

Firstly some useful advice on days in the month (forget the rhyme). All over the Middle East they just clench both hands and count the knuckles and the spaces in between. Knuckles are the 31 day months so from the left January, March and May have 31 days and then you go to August onto the other hand with 31 days and so on. The rest between have 30 and we can all remember February which normally has 28. As they say problem solved and throw that silly old rhyme out of the window!

People

30th September
We can be justly proud of our Heritage centre. Not only the exhibits but the building itself are a part old Uttoxeter. We can only imagine Francis Redfern working in his spare time in those same rooms in 1881 between making barrels as a cooper. Digging out old documents to seek out what actually did take place in Uttoxeter during the Civil War over 200 years before – then kindly asking the public for their favourable reception to his great work which had taken him 27 years to complete!

It has been my pleasure this week to start work on the new Heritage Centre DVD with Peter Nixon the curator. I am sure we shall end up with something which will add to the interest for all who visit the centre.

30th September
Gordon Bradley
I wonder how many of you were able to see Gordon Bradley's flower arranging demonstration last week at the Town Hall. It is amazing what he has managed to achieve from his shop in Church Street over the years including of course flowers for the Royal Family. Yes his anthuriums did not pass unnoticed by the guests during the Princess Royal's recent visit. Long may you continue the good work Gordon despite rumours you may be thinking of retirement.

30th September
The team at Elkes Biscuits.
We have all noticed their new store off Brookside Road and wondered just how

many biscuits are in there and just what the size of their operation is – all requiring to be of first class quality conforming to modern standards.

Well I understand they produce an incredible 1000 tons/per week. I couldn't resist working this out examining an average packet of biscuits. This came to an enormous weekly pile 50 ft high by 50 ft square at the base. (15M by 15M by 15M if you want metric). All this before taking the opportunity of opening the packet and passing them round!

31st October
Betty and Bernard Wilks
I would like to pay tribute to Uttoxeter's twice past mayor Betty Wilks and her husband Bernard. Betty has always been a fighter for the town and has not enjoyed the best of health and health recently, nor I regret has her husband Bernard, whom some of you might remember was also a councillor. There is more to the town council than just politics.

31st October
Charles Brogden, visit of young people from Montenegro
I was delighted to attend a conference of young people on Saturday organised by Charles Brogden (Staffs Youth and Community Service) with the young people from Montenegro held at the racecourse by kind permission of John Iveson. Our young people from Uttoxeter were well represented. As you may know Charles is setting up a Youth Forum (if you are interested phone him on 07968373281) and Kirsty Jones is organising a meeting for young people to meet councillors within the next few weeks. Well done to all who took part and we hope our friends from Montenegro take back with them happy memories of our town.

20th November
Ronald McDonald
Our thanks to Ronald McDonald, our town crier, the Town Hall team and to all who gave raffle prizes for the children, and to those who blew up the balloons for a successful switch on of the lights starting our run up to Christmas. Thanks again of course to Len Woodward and his team for putting them up – fitting the lamps with the aid of a motorised 'cherry picker' was an impressive sight in itself. Our decision to return the Christmas tree to the market place is to some extent an act of faith (and of CCTV!) I hope all will be well and it will prove a worthy focus for the town's celebrations.

29th November
David Hewitt and Wilfred Johnson

Whilst walking or driving along one of our by-ways have you noticed those footpath finger posts? You fancy a walk across the field but are concerned you might wander off the track and upset the farmer or worse those bulls are scary!

To clear things I went along to talk to David Hewitt. It is David with Wilfred Johnson who have done so much to keep that happy balance between the struggling farmer and us Uttoxeter townies who would like to enjoy the countryside but don't want to upset anybody doing it. This is what I learnt:

In the old days when the old boys wandered to work over the fields there was plenty of space around the crops, they walked round the edges amongst the wild flowers. There would still be no problem even with the slightly unsteady return from the pub, but not any more. As well as finger posts and stiles required for each road crossing David is trying with the help of the County Council to waymark the routes across the fields. By defining the routes exactly crop damage can be minimised and, by erecting signs to remind ramblers to respect the countryside, to reduce the inevitable clash between the rambler and the farmer.

Yes, over past centuries the needs of the working man in Uttoxeter was a path to the farm where he mostly worked, one to the pub to see his mates in the evening and one to get to church with his wife on Sundays. We think we have come a long way since then with a more balanced family life. As we struggle with the jams along the A50 do we spare a thought for the labyrinth of byways and footpaths which still crisscross our countryside?

To preserve some order all these footpaths where they appeared on maps were frozen as rights of way in the Access to Countryside Act of 1949. As a result there are an almost unbelievable 8,500 miles of these in Staffordshire alone. At the same time as encouraging us to use them, we need also to keep us respectful of the countryside, remembering that farmers have a difficult enough time to survive these days without ramblers adding unnecessarily to their problems.

In addition they also impact on new developments where rights of way need to be changed, in these cases someone needs to speak up for the countryside.

As well as the Staffordshire Way which runs through our area, David reminded me that we also have a circular footpath route which runs all around the town. You don't need to walk it all, various sections can be taken separately and David has promised to have a good route map (with his famous illustrations) available in the new year from the Heritage Centre and the Advice Bureau behind the Town Hall showing you the way.

I know there are rules about these things but there is no substitute for respect on both sides and a bit of give and take – so if you want to know more or you would like to join the ramblers Wilfred would be pleased to talk to you on 563320. Enjoy our countryside – it is worth saving!

30th November
Steve Dayman and Steve Fear

A postscript to the Meningitis walk, if you remember Steve Dayman and Steve Fear walked through the town on 14th October on their round Britain (22 miles per day) walk. They made an incredible £85,000 from sponsorship, donations and collections from this walk alone. Thanks again to all including the Lions who helped them.

7th Febuary
John Cooper and Peter Nixon

It was also a pleasure this week to visit the Heritage Centre to thank John Cooper and Peter Nixon for their part in the new introduction video. I should like also to wish John and Brenda Cooper all the best for their forthcoming retirement from the electrical business. Many of you will remember Brenda as a very vigorous ex Town Mayor and supporter of Town Twinning!

9th March
Denise Leigh

It is not often someone special performs in Uttoxeter and then takes off as a national star! Denise Leigh has done just this. On the first of this month she was bringing tears to our eyes at the Viennese evening in the Town Hall singing the Laughing Song by Johann Strauss – this week she was smiling again – on TV having a good time with the others on the bus on en route to the national finals of 'Operatunity.'

Then to be acclaimed as joint winner was very special. She was described by the expert judges as being 'vocally and histrionically exceptional.' Not sure what this means but well done Denise, we are pleased to be part of your success. Of course you are blind so thanks especially to your supportive family for making it possible for us all to enjoy your very special talent.

9th March
Paul Moretti

Recently I had a visit from Paul Moretti who wants to start a boxing club in town. My first reaction was that boxing is an outdated dangerous sport and I suppose most of you would agree with this. However so is the taking of dangerous drugs, this might have some appeal if there is any evidence that taking up the sport might prevent even some of our young people shortening their lives with the habit. So just for now I'm sitting on the ropes with this one but there have been a few local surprises.

Strange facts emerge when you delve into local history. Apparently Uttoxeter was once the very centre of boxing in Staffordshire. Yes we all know of Bartley our world champion (he's remembered with affection on the millennium monument) but what of the boxing club which used to thrive in town, the training gym in George Bladen's Wool Staplers on Bridge Street which became the Green Bus Company then Angus MacKinnon's test bay, then after the war up over the Red Lion (now the Lion Buildings), of joint promotions in the Queen's Hall and the Town Hall, of boxing booths at the fair, of Tom Hodkinson, of Fred Bloor, of Len Bailey and of Lal Shepherd and of rumours on blindfold boxing (surely not). It's all a can of worms –

15th March
Jack Jardine and more on Uttoxeter boxing
For more of past boxing in the town it was my pleasure to go along to meet that crafty old codger Jack Jardine.

He gave me more on Len Bailey the knockout specialist – he had to be – the story goes that on the night he would quaff his pints in the Wellington with boxing shorts under his trousers. When advised by his runner that his fight was due, he left his pint foaming but unfinished. Repairing quickly to the Town Hall he would KO his hapless opponent swiftly it was said in time to

return to finish the beer not yet flat on the bar!

There was Piper Crutchley a curious possibly devious type sporting a bow tie. He followed the wakes on a bike first Ashbourne then Ucheter on to Burton then to Coalville each time in the boxing booth to fight all comers – standing up to anyone who fancied knocking him down a peg or two for a prize of £1.

What I could not understand from Jack was how come when they all fought in the Town Hall as amateurs (no face guards and big gloves in those days) he said they needed to be hungry and penniless to fancy a fight, I guess there was a pay-off somewhere but thought it wise not to ask. Keep going old timer!*

21st March
Galya Bisaengaliev

To report on another sell-out notable performance at the Town Hall! This time it was the Friends of St Mary's presenting Galya Bisengaliev a pianist from Kazakhstan now living in UK who was ably supported by the Denstone Swing Band. The audience were amazed by the sheer skill of Galya, my only regret was that councillors at the Council Meeting upstairs were allowed to hear only her final applause – well done Galya.

26th April
Harry Shaw

Walking down Carter Street the other day I looked up at the archway leading to Saddler's Yard for the first time in years and noticed Harry Shaw's notice had gone. Harry you may remember knew absolutely everybody and made his duty so to do. His haircuts were short and military exactly to the fashion of the farmer and there were many more of those in the early 80's. His shop was a small room on the right hand side you waited in 'sit up and beg' benches close to Harry who chatted away on the gossip of the day.

I prided myself in sitting there quiet – for in those days I was there for a desert cut. This was just the thing before taking off for another session in the sand. I noticed the old boys from the farms, they kept their greasy flat hats on, even in the shop – only taking them off to expose their white scalps for the clippers. When all done it was caps on and off outside back to normal all covered up as if nothing had happened. Back in the desert during each session I needed one haircut so I went into the local town called Beda Zayed. True they gave you coffee, which you never got at Harry's, but again I watched the locals,

---

* with regret to learn that Jack Jardine died later in the year.

43

same thing really but their local headgear was the Arab kaffeyeh. Only when in the chair off it came – first the snake bit that kept it on, then the red and white squared cloth, then off with a skull cap under, nice head of hair exposed, on with the clippers, back on with it all, then out of the shop, again as if nothing had happened.

3rd May
Len Woodward
We have a neurotic church spire weathercock this morning – dizzy from being buzzed round and round in and out of the clouds by a determined Cessna plane dragging a large notice 'Len Woodwards 60th'. A sparking performance this, best wishes to you Len, may your cables never be crossed.

3rd May
Bill and Marjorie Tranter
It was my pleasure this week to go along to Rocester to meet Bill and Marjorie Tranter. Bill has been doing very active local charity work for no less than 38 years. The Air ambulance, Katherine House, Highfield Hall, millennium project, Rocester interdenominational war memorial and many other charities have benefited from their charity work. They put in many hours each week at the village hall where Bill is Chairman now made self sufficient on running costs following charity status. Always up to something to raise money they are into everything from bingo calling to large scale plastic duck racing. I am proud to endorse the rumour that they are both invited to a garden party at Buckingham Palace in July. Splendid efforts well recognised and endorsed by their perky miniature cockatoo Joey who refused to perform his talking or barking routine during my visit.

Developments

30th September
Uttoxeter Plus
Well done Peter Ross for getting final approval for our Implementation Plan.

One problem is getting the message over to certain very busy people who could benefit.

I know he is concerned to get into touch particularly with small businesses who have ideas to expand in areas of High Tech (usually computer/software related), food, or tourism. If the facts are right grant aid is available.

If you know someone beavering away long hours at a small business with no time to get informed of our initiatives with Uttoxeter Plus please pass on the message. It may be do their advantage and we are only here to help.

We also support Peter in the work he is doing to promote tourism. Going back again to the time of the civil war, the town's history at that time is certainly one which is of great interest to all and excellent for attracting visitors.

Local residents (being traders and farmers they made expert diplomats) declared for neither side and even provided a deputation to Charles I demanding (one supposes by asking nicely) that he sue for peace with the parliamentary forces.

I believe something may be on with the Sealed Knot Society for an event down the racecourse. How appropriate this would be as it was at this very spot down by the town meadows that the parliamentary armies encamped whilst plundering the town for supplies. This was typically the order for the day for soldiers but the locals, again showing talent for this kind of situation, were able to successfully sue for compensation!

30th September
Centre of Excellence

I expect all football supporters will be looking forward to seeing the new football centre of excellence under construction at 5 lane ends. Particularly with the delays in replacing our national stadium this is being heralded as a key to possible success for our national team for the next World Cup.

17th October
Cemetery Chapels

You will be glad to know that contractors have quietly started work on the Cemetery Chapels after the huge financial hurdles were overcome. We keep our fingers crossed for a successful outcome I know the determination to succeed is there with Geoff Morrison and his team. We shall do our level best to give them our full support.

20th November
Peter Ross, Uttoxeter Plus

From what I hear nearly all of you were disappointed to hear of the resignation of Peter Ross our Uttoxeter Plus Manager. You will be pleased to know that Borough Council Regeneration and Partnerships are actively helping to fill this gap with advertisements in the press and hopefully interviews before Christmas.

20th November
Cemetery Chapels
Works continue to go smoothly on the Cemetery Chapels. The ring beams necessary to prevent further movement of the walls are due to be cast this week. The team at a recent meeting are now sorting out the best method of heating and internal details for opening next spring – good luck to them!

18th January
Cemetery
Last month I refered to the good progress being made on the cemetery chapels and that the next move was to tackle the urgent housekeeping improvements to the grounds, to improve things in a sensible cost-efficient manner. As many of you will know from the national press we are now obliged by law to take steps to make the area safe following a number of accidents to children countrywide. To this end we are very anxious to think out our strategy properly before starting any testing programme.

13th January
Heart Resuscitation Unit
You know success is not all about money and this was proved last week following great efforts to get the first defib. (heart resuscitation) unit on the ground here in Uttoxeter. It was my greatest pleasure to attend the handover of the first unit to the Leisure Centre. A real milestone for the town and a signpost for the future.

Thanks to the efforts of the Lions team headed by David Allen we shall soon, after some final training, be having a life saving unit available on site. Denise Meadows and Paul Bryan said the following on this very important subject:

'It is reassuring for all our customers to know that this vital piece of life saving equipment will shortly be available at the Leisure Centre. We are very pleased to be chosen by the Lions to receive this state of the art defibrillator which will be soon be in the reception area readily on hand for the use of our trained personnel. Staffordshire Ambulance Service will be delivering initial training on the equipment to 12 members of our staff in early February with regular 3 monthly sessions thereafter. We should like to thank the Uttoxeter Lions for their kind donation of this vital piece of equipment and also for their support in setting up the equipment and sorting out the training.' Well done to all concerned, I am sure that further details will be available when the unit comes officially on line.

I am very happy indeed to name the people who have made this possible:

From the Lions David Allen (he will not want me to say this but he's already saved a life with one of these units) and his colleagues Robert Sunderland and Ken Baxter under their President Tony Dallison and from the Leisure Centre at the caring sharp end will be Angela Brunt, Stephanie Edge, Sarah Clayton, Paul Bryan (Marketing Manager), Mark Oakes (Operations Manager), and Janie Stubbs. Overseeing and giving essential instruction was Nigel Sherman from Staffs Ambulance Service – you all have our full support.

Please let this not be the end of the story. Around here excepting the Leisure Centre these units are available only to the paramedics, St Johns and the Red Cross. As you can guess speed is of the essence to save lives and I'm afraid we are well behind the times. In the USA they are almost obligatory in all public places and JCB always in the forefront of these things have 3 such units at Rocester. I am told that supermarkets and High Street stores are the best places, anyone interested please get into touch with the Lions, if the will is there I am sure we can get the money together in one way or another. All success to this venture

15th February
Town Hall

Of course we need more of such events in our Town Hall and I was slightly concerned to hear various premature comments concerning its future. However the message is clear – we are serious about reducing costs and, our priority now is to find alternatives to bring the building into better use be it more functions, one stop shop, commercial letting/leasing, or looking at reducing the rates which are estimated for next year at no less than £19,300. The building has been much renovated and we have open minds on its medium term future but the present situation where it is 25% empty with too little income through functions is clearly not acceptable. However present talks to improve the utilisation of the building with the Borough, County Council and others have barely begun and no concrete proposals are yet on the table.

22nd February
Uttoxeter Plus

Uttoxeter Plus is alive and well! Of course things never go quickly enough as far as I'm concerned but five submissions for the design of our new Town Centre Master Plan have now been received and assessment is about to start. The idea is kick off with outside expert advice – after all we are not the first in this business. Then we can take it from there in local discussion before getting it onto the books as planning guidance. The result is a document to guide and encourage developers to get on with the job. We must show that we mean business. As important are parallel initiatives for small businesses assistance, and a survey of available commercial sites.

1st March
Uttoxeter Furnishing/United Reform Church

All sorts of interesting things turned up when Uttoxeter Furnishing closed after so many years – the place is to be turned into a café, wine bar and club. Something to be encouraged I am sure for what is now refered to as the 'night time economy.' (I must say I never thought of it quite in these terms in the old days) Anyway as the plaque on the entrance quite clearly says it was the site of the Independent Chapel, started in 1792 which later moved out to Carter Street during the latter part of the 19th century and is now known as the United Reform Church. These good people are interested on any information from local families whose relatives attended the original chapel in the old days – in particular any old records on 'hatchings, matchings and dispatchings.'

15th March
A50 Crossing

First good news on the pedestrian crossings at the junction of the A50 and the B5030 (Ashbourne Road, Rocester Road). We are advised that improved paving, signage and guard-railing is soon to be provided for the two uncontrolled pedestrian crossings plus additional road markings advising pedestrians of vehicles turning into the A50 service entrance. We have been concerned about this for some time now with the increasing traffic using this slip road for petrol and drive-in snacks.

15th March
Scrap Yards off A50

Whilst we are in this area all is still not quite well. We put restrictions on new enterprises like the quarry to minimise the impact on the neighbourhood – they remove over 1000T per week of gravel from the site and hold regular meetings with the public to minimise their impact – all very creditable.

At the same time why can't we ask the Barlows and the Bloors politely to operate their scrap businesses in a way which is less offensive. At present mountains of grotesque, twisted metal protrude above the fence surrounding the Esso Garage and MacDonalds like an invading army. Not only does this appear to me not to make particular commercial sense but this is an appalling eyesore at a gateway to the town. Without going through the tedious legal procedures why can't we wish them well in their very necessary operations but ask them out of ordinary common decency to either reduce the height of the scrap piles or simply make an arrangement to raise the fence so that their operation is not visible to the public?

21st March
Uttoxeter Plus

A milestone for the town occurred this week when Taylor Young, GVA Grimley were appointed consultants by Uttoxeter Plus for the Town's Masterplan and Delivery Strategy. We met Stephen Gleave, Andrea Key and Andrew Clarke with Philip Summerfield from Borough Planning to discuss first details.

The baseline will be the consultations already completed as part of the Health Check last year. The 20 week programme will give planning advice combining urban and landscape design with realistic development advice. The area covered is bounded by the railway on the south (including the station), to the east roughly by the bypass, to the north by a line crossing the end of the High street and to the west by a line along the west side of the cattle market.

The big reassurance for me was that the outcome would not just be a 'pie in the sky' architect's dream but would combine modern principles of urban design with some measure of known commercial choice in the kinds of development best for the town. We know there is a good demand for 4 or 5 bedroom houses and this is being well developed but what we need to find out from the experts is how we can develop community areas, retail improvements where necessary in the town centre and affordable housing. They will complete the project in three stages with a further consultation event following stage 2.

Uttoxeter Plus would like to receive more suggestions and ideas from the rural sectors.

12th April
Confusion on the High Street

Whilst digging the garden on Saturday morning a message came through that there was some confusion on the High Street – so I went across to witness District Officer Johnson and Special Constable Bostock dealing with those cars which contrary to the current Traffic Order were being driven down the High Street. A fairly spectacular scene unfolded with cars queuing up (locked in the one-way system) to be suitably admonished and deservedly so. Our High Street is for the safe passage of pedestrians during daylight hours as the sign clearly shows. However what is so frustrating is when we know the simple solution is now available (in the form of retractable remotely operated bollards) I believe the money is available, they already have this system going in Tamworth and other places – yet for us it takes such a time to get done. A price has been sought this past three months now that I know of. It will be so much safer particularly for mothers with young children and will allow controlled street selling and a more relaxed environment for young and old alike.

19th April
New Housing for New and old Residents
With the A50 and the bypass more and more people now want to live in Uttoxeter. We should not be surprised at this but it brings with it the need for better facilities whilst keeping the essential character of the town which people like. Already we have in the planning process at one stage or another no less than four applications for 2 and 3 storey town-house type apartments all on 'brown-field' sites within easy walking distance of the town centre. These are behind Bradley Street (now in process of construction), further down the High Street (on the J & E Fabrications site), off Town Meadows Way (on the Roebuck site) and further along Town Meadows way opposite Tescos. These represent well over 200 apartments some of the starter homes type. Whether these end up as what is described as 'affordable' depends as always on how many eventually are owned by Housing Associations. Quite a thought this and it does not include housing which might be included on the cattle market site.

This is happening because people want to come to live here. It is certainly presents a challenge to ensure these developments are made for the good of the town including all the new facilities that will need to go with it.

Local Events

19th October
Lighting the War Memorial
As a postscript to the switching on of the war memorial lights I should like to thank the West Midlands Regiment for once again turning out so efficiently with so little fuss with their famous mascot Watchman 4. He is a magnificent black Staffordshire Bull Terrier – you will be pleased to know he is shortly to be promoted from his present rank (lance-corporal) for faithful services rendered!

Also the police again with their force of specials made us all safe from traffic danger, including some of us who are not so young as we used to be. Many thanks to them. I believe they are looking for more volunteers as specials. These public-spirited men and women give four hours free per week after an initial training period of six months. It is not surprising that a number of local specials have decided on a career in the force which unfortunately has left the specials with vacancies. So why not join them, we all feel proud of the number of those in town who are prepared to give their time to community service in one way or another.

In these so-called enlightened days community service is considered by the general public as a punishment in lieu of a jail sentence – I believe it should be a looked at as a voluntary duty for those who are able.

Also for the Staffs CC lighting engineers who did so well in designing the lights. I never realised what a difference a subtle change in colour can make – well done also to them!

19th October

Potamus – no relation to Nostradamus, it's not about predicting the future, it's about the present. It's about a friendly hippo introducing walking buses for children going to school. We have already one here in town from the end of Balance Hill to Picknalls and hopefully another can soon be started along Holly Road to St Mary's.

We were discussing this last week as part of 'Safer Routes to School.' So what is the connection? Well it's all about reducing the number of cars at the school gates and improving the health of our children.

Of course children living far away come by bus and the schools take much care and trouble getting these children safety into school but with our school access roads dating from the 19th century the congestion outside the gates before and after school gets worse every year.

There is always danger in crossing roads and 'walking buses' need to be properly supervised. In the end it comes down to parent's co-operation but why not give it a try, it has the full backing of Staffs Education. Other points of concern which were noted for action on the roads for parents with children were:

- the danger crossing the end of Kingfisher Way or Stafford Road to link with the Old Knotty Way pelican crossing
- after going across the A50 via the splendid new crossings, the danger crossing the uncontrolled sliproad with cars swinging round to access MacDonalds or the petrol station.

30th October
Christmas Celebrations
Hopefully we will have a good big Christmas tree this year thanks to the Borough Council's kind offer. I know many people would like to see it again in the market place where it should be for the carols and good Christmas cheer and I'm all for this. However we shall take the advice of the police – like all of us they deserve a good Christmas and they are only reflecting the way things are today, but watch this space!

As for the lights tell the children we are looking everywhere for the famous Ronald MacDonald with his magic tricks to see if he will come to Uttoxeter to switch on our Christmas lights at 5pm on 15th November. He is surprisingly difficult to catch as he goes so quickly on those huge shoes but if we catch him listen out for the town crier earlier in the day along the High Street crying out the good news.

9th November
A Brighter Spring
Very pleased indeed to see that Uttoxeter in Bloom is heading the charge for an even brighter springtime for the town next year! With help gratefully accepted from our schools we should have thousands of new bulbs planted in our verges to give the town that extra cheery look for spring.

9th November
An even Bigger Rocket
Seeing all the spectacular fireworks last week reminded me of one night in St Petersburg, that's the one with all the mod. cons on the west coast of Florida. Knowing the exact time of launch of the shuttle from the Kennedy Space Centre almost exactly 150 miles away on the opposite coast, I wandered outside just to see on the off chance if anything was visible.

It was disappointing and something of an anticlimax when at the appointed time nothing happened! Knowing how vital launch time was I didn't wait long, I guess around 4 minutes, before returning to the hotel to get back to bed. In front of the hotel steps I turned round to have a last look and there was this amazing flaming exhaust rising straight up into the sky clearly visible from all those miles away. The shuttle then turned gently over into orbit and as if this were not enough turned as if by magic into a bright shining star as it came out of the earth's shadow.

It's all a matter of scale and this was awesome – doing a bit of geometry to do with the curvature of the earth the shuttle needed to be nearly 3 miles high before it could be seen from St Petes' and that was the reason for the time lag, to the same scale it was just like us seeing the fireworks on the Thames Embankment from Bramshall Park!

11th November
A Prizegiving
It was my pleasure to attend Thomas Alleynes prizegiving on Wednesday. Again our students did well in their exams and other activities, they remain a credit to their parents, their teachers and the three school system we have available for most students in the town. I make no apology in repeating again that they may stand up and be counted against any school in the land.

On a practical note the school is in the centre of town and there is a fair interaction between the school and the town's shoppers and traders. To retain the present good relations the school did confirm that they prefer to be advised directly of any problems so they can take action accordingly.

11th November
A Postscript to Remembrance Day
This year on remembrance day those who were able remembered fallen comrades from the past and now we look to the next three months with some apprehension as war danger time in Iraq approaches. In the middle east the daytime sun now is lower in the sky, cooler winds blow and western soldiers and their electronics are able to go to war in this place to fight for freedom.

20th November
Christmas celebrations
So we have started on the run up to Christmas! I know we always say it starts earlier each year but we have so few feast days compared with our European friends we need to make the very most of what we have.

A big thank-you to Ronald McDonald for switching on the lights last Friday he was as always a big attraction for the children. Our town crier was also in attendance together with the town hall team who blew up the balloons so most children had one together with their first Christmas sweetie. Full marks also to Len Woodward and his team who have done a splendid job and our town clerk who has ensured we comply with all the new regulations.

I hope our decision to return the Christmas tree to the market place proves a successful focus once again for our town's celebrations – it is good to see we have now that CCTV camera to show up any wrongdoings!

15th December
Christmas, drugs and help

At Christmas if we are lucky we have the chance to come together amongst family and old friends to get up to date with the latest news – and try to video all those good films on the telly for watching later!

For those not so lucky Christmas tends also to focus on the negative side of things from loneliness to crime to drugs and I've tried this week to find out more about what is being done and what more can be done.

We started off in our small way by talking about the Christmas tree in the market place with Inspector Andy Mason. Nearly everyone wants to keep it up until twelfth night but New Year's Eve is a problem – so far so good but remember that if we are forced to take action during the holidays some poor guys from Community Services will be asked to give up part of their holiday to take it away. So please give the police a call if you see anyone messing about with it in the meantime.

Then we talked with Donna Meredith-Wood the Borough Council's Community Safety Manager about the town's growing problems with drugs. Hard drugs are an issue in Uttoxeter. In Staffordshire you might be surprised to know that no less than 199 people were dealt with by the Police for supplying 'class A' hard drugs last year. Of course the first part about solving any problem is finding the facts and an audit has now been done for this very purpose. The Community Safety Partnership has a Substance Misuse task group to tackle these very problems. This group is chaired by Donna and includes representatives from the Police, the Drug Action Team, Integrated Drug and Alcohol Services, Social services and Probation.

It's no good at all us oldies being do-gooders, not only were we never tempted in our younger days but it is our generation who have now allowed this menace into our society. I know I was blind to the danger when I saw it all in the 80s in Columbia. Then we joked about the law of the gun, the plantations of forbidden substances and the open sale over there in the street, never believing some of it could come here. Well I'm afraid it has.

However let the older generation take some reassurance as it is the young apparently who are most often the victims of drug related crime.

Christmas time also tends to act as a focus on family problems and being positive the Domestic Violence Protection Committee has set up a domestic abuse helpline on 01283 536006 in time for the festive season. Counselling mostly means listening – the aim is to give help, support and advice where it is required. Good luck to all who are involved in this. Another bit of advice is to watch out for car crime, keep those presents locked away out of sight away from prying eyes. Our pleasure is their opportunity.

The concept of Community Safety is a partnership of action groups coordinating the approach between the police, the Health Care Trusts, the schemes for youth offenders, the drugs action team and the fire service. Please take note of their telephone number for help 01283 508626.

18th January
Thomas Alleynes Achievements

The greatest pleasure this week has been to attend Thomas Alleyne's Senior Prize Giving. Those who left last term had kindly returned to the school to receive their prizes for achievement in the presence of teachers, parents and guests.

It was a chance for them to record their final school achievements and for us to wish them all the best for their future careers, helped by some timely, amusing and appropriate advice from the guest of honour Mr Bob Morley, very well known to all leavers as former Deputy Head and Head of Sixth form – all about both working hard and having that hinterland of other interests outside of career and family which makes life worth while. I guess his jokes which were mostly concerned with his teaching experiences since his official retirement should be considered as copyright!

At the same time Headteacher Mr Peter Mitchell was able to list the achievements of the school, an 'A' level pass rate of 99% with 48% A grades speaks for itself but exam results of course are not everything. I was impressed by the willingness amongst the teaching staff to take what he described as 'calculated risks' outside the basic curriculum to achieve that bit of extra understanding which in the end often makes the difference.

Well done Thomas Alleyne's. As was said these things are not bound to happen. It is a combination of things – the initial product from first and second schools, and contributions from teachers, parents and governors all with a real determination to help our young people. Of course we must all improve for the future but I say again I believe just now our young people in Uttoxeter can stand up proudly against any others in this land.

7th Febuary
Crime in Uttoxeter

On saturday it was our pleasure to go along to Wilfred House to talk to Victor Littleford, Alan Felthouse and Dennis Browne at the coffee morning organised by Neighbourhood Watch.

I certainly found I needed bringing up to date on the latest spate of organised crimes against the home which are affecting even us here in Uttoxeter – although as a fairly well knit community please remember we are far down the list of the worst areas for this kind of crime.

We talked about bogus callers, we all know about the bogus salesman, water man, builder or gardener and the need to ask for proper identity and to make a prior appointment to be sure, but what about that teary-eyed young girl who wants to use the phone or the toilet then lets in someone else to do the dirty work? I find this kind to thing difficult to believe but it does happen. Apparently it is mostly drug related so we all need to be on our guard.

To combat this kind to crime there is the chain and a mirror on the door to see better who is calling – if you feel that you are elderly or vulnerable or just worried what might happen you can get help from Victim Support, Trent and Dove Housing if you are their tenant, or if you ring the numbers as below. All this is done under the guidance of the police.

The firm recommendation is to report all such crimes to the police without delay. This is most important, they are there to give advice. The last thing you want is for either it to happen again or for any such incident to affect your life. Even if you are not sure if something was taken or perhaps you think you have lost it yourself, or it might turn up sometime – ring the police they are there to help.

By the way there is a new initiative this year for drugs awareness in schools. We have been fortunate these past years to have the services of Paul Betts. Now this function will be carried on by Ian Hall and we wish him all the very best in his new role of talking to local schools, some of you will already know him from his previous role as Schools Liaison Officer.

15th February
RNLI concert in Town Hall
It was our pleasure last Saturday to join a packed Town Hall for a Viennese evening by the Stafford Sinfonia. This was conducted by Darrell Wade in aid of the RNLI organised by our own Uttoxeter Lifeboat Guild. Denise Leigh once again brought tears to our eyes by her rendering of the Laughing Song by Johann Strauss as did Jonathan Baddeley's sensitive notes on the 2 by 2 angle iron during the Anvil Polka by the same composer. As if this were not sufficient there was the finale by the audience at the conclusion of the Emperor Waltz played on various party poppers tuned specially for the occasion. A very good time indeed was had by all present!

A little on the Lifeboat Guild presently led by Joyce Woodhead, Sally Herbert and Muriel Maude. The Guild has been running for around 35 years following a visit from a certain Col. Benn. He certainly started things splendidly. Despite our Guild having the UK prize for being the furthest away from any lifeboat they have since flourished and have contributed in excess of £50,000 to RNLI funds! This including £400 recently from a sponsored private coffee-supported knit-in, blankets produced went to the local baby unit – very well done to all concerned. The Guild meet each month at the Robin Hood at Bramshall.

20th Febuary
Battle of Uttoxeter
Other good news is that a start has been made on preparations for the Battle of Uttoxeter. We can be justly proud of this event as it formed a milestone in British history when in 1648 there was made here in Uttoxeter a first step towards the kind of government we have today – and more important whether you will support John Lambert (a good move) or the Marquis of Hamilton (an unfortunate choice as it turned out) for two great days of entertainment down the racecourse the 19th and 20th July! Our thanks to everyone including John Iveson the General Manager and all others concerned at the racecourse for their co-operation.

1st March
Crime
I am sure the thing to do is not to get upset by the obnoxious few. After the weekend we had a continuation of this spate of smashed windows, attention

being turned to telephone boxes down Carter Street and Hockley Road. Look out for anyone in possession of an emergency window break glass hammer for no good reason. We are in discussion with the police on this matter and have no sympathies at all with those concerned.

1st March
Pennycroft Park

As if this were not enough on our public parks it was my pleasure to attend the opening of the new facilities at Pennycroft Park on wednesday. This is so important as a green area for residents of properties on Park Street and thereabouts. The new toddlers play area, the 9 – 13's facilities and the arena are all first class. Again thanks to the Borough for the finance and well done Parks Department. Now we need to go further with the football pitches (the only public ones in town), and for new toilets and changing facilities. Never to forget as well the need for equipment for Mary Howitt Playsafe Park on Howitt Crescent. There is no reason at all why this part of the town should lag behind.

1st March
Uttoxeter's Inner Wheel

Another pleasure was to attend our Uttoxeter Inner Wheel's 58th Birthday Fellowship held at JCB Lakeside Club at the invitation of Sally Herbert their president. Their recent purchase with Rotary of a 'light writer' for communicating with serious stroke victims was certainly something else new to me. There was an excellent turnout from other local groups to hear David Tideswell again on garden birds. David is a bit like marmite and I'm one of those who can't get enough of his enthusiasm for his subject! The quick-fire way he answers those difficult questions with yet another burst of information I find quite fascinating, as my old friend says 'you can go birding anywhere, in a traffic jam on the motorway, waiting for a bus, on a walk or more especially from your kitchen window.' David once again well done you entertained us all splendidly.

9th March
Battle of Uttoxeter

Not all is good news however. Due to some last minute problems at the racecourse and finances not being cleared it looks as if the Battle of Uttoxeter will have to be postponed for this year. The slightly cynical might say that the re-enactment of an important non-event is also to be a non-event!

9th March
Uttoxeter Plus
More good progress now that we, with the help of the Borough Council, have a professional outside consultant lined up for our Town Masterplan to be used for planning guidance. The basic local consultation has been completed. This should supply that additional input to bring it all together based on best experience from elsewhere. Unfortunately the time scale is 20 weeks and again we are in waiting mode. However on the positive side the ground work has been done, now we need that special flair from the experts. The other two current Uttoxeter Plus projects – the assistance for small businesses and the review of commercial sites are both going ahead. So if you are a small business look out for the details.

15th March
PDSA Charity Shop
We were pleased to attend the reopening of the PDSA shop in the market place. Carol Woolley who manages the shop advised us that this place alone contributes over £100,000 per year to the PDSA . I was also very pleased to hear that some of this cash is made available at the local vets in the form of PetAid for all those on benefits or income support (within the ST14 postcode area) to help with their vet bills – good for people as well as pets. Like all similar shops they are always on the lookout for volunteers, notwithstanding long service awards I was pleased to present to Mary Owen, Beryl Holley and Ida Deakin.

21st March
'It's Your Shout'
I was pleased to be present at Carlton Televisions 'It's your Shout' on 9th March. I thought all involved made the event a credit and an excellent advertisement for the town. Many thanks to all who were present.

12th April
A Winter's Tale
This week a typically bold and imaginative move by Thomas Alleynes High School brought Shakespeare's 'The Winter's Tale' to Uttoxeter. The plot being unknown to me and somewhat obscure I was left to enjoy those great one-liners, Richard Castle giving a fine performance as the King of Sicilia (he left immediately after the performance to tour World War 1 battlefields in France – well done Richard) and Richard Curtis doing his part as Antigonus, multi-skilled, he's going in for engineering – good for you Richard. Most impressive seeing the

whole team pulling together under Ian Lewis having rehearsed even saturdays and sundays to produce a theme of words and spectacle. I am sure those who participated will remember this for many years to come.

I'll say once again our young people in Uttoxeter are able to stand proud against any in this land. The one liners? Some of these were set out in their well contrived programme – how about the suggestive 'your actions are my dreams,' or possibly the polite but firm 'I like your silence' or even 'I have drunk and seen the spider' (which I unfortunately misheard 'as I am drunk I saw the spider')

19th April
The union flag

We fly the union flag this week on the Town Hall at your request and out of respect for all our local men and women in the armed forces and others for whatever reason presently out in the Gulf. Good luck to you, may this war now end quickly so you may return safe to your families.

19th April
Clubnight at the Town Hall

It is easy to say that here in town we have nowhere for young people to go, ignoring what is on offer and the people who are doing their very best for youth. This week we had over 100 young people at 'Clubnight at the Town Hall.' The place really hummed with electronic computer generated music, strobe lights and a brilliant athletic performance of street and breakdance routines by Uttoxeter Flava. This had followed 'workshop' sessions lead by Michele Clerc at the Cellar Youth Club and Oldfelds Youth Club, sponsored by the Borough Council Community Arts Programme. Well done by all concerned special thanks to Carl Woolley quietly keeping overall control as always (can you believe he has worked 32 years for young people) with Frank Alsop, Geoff Lavick, Gary Hamblin, Simon Danks, Maggie Collins, and Collette Wain. As an oldie I was way out of my depth with my insides vibrating with the noise but great to be with you – thanks also to the Red Cross who were kindly in attendance.

19th April
Charity Ferret Racing?

One of my more unusual assignments this week was to investigate reports of an outbreak of charity ferret racing down Dove Bank. Lots of fun was had I believe. The advice I received was that the outbreak may be stopped by sliding a 1 M long by 50mm diameter tube down the offender's trousers along with a piece of chocolate confiscated from winnings – alternatively dispersal for the Easter holidays!

19th April
Coffee Morning – Old People's Welfare
We had the pleasure of attending the Wilfred House coffee morning organised by the Old Peoples' Welfare Committee. I do like chatting about old Uttoxeter – there is always someone with a new tale to tell. Thanks to the team of Betty Harrison, Shielia Devine, Viv Adshead, Brenda Cole, Barbara Burton, Georgina Barrett and Margaret Gradwell for once again organising things. A difficulty is always contacting people who would like to come for a chat, if you see a notice I suppose a kind thing to do is to contact someone who you know might like to come, all are welcome.

19th April
Our troops in Iraq/Saddam Hussain
With all the mass of instant TV reports sometimes confusing the issue I believe we should remember the simple fact that this cruel dictator survived for 24 years ruling a country with the second highest oil reserves in the world. He started his evil ways in 1980 by invading Iran for rich pickings at a time when the country was in turmoil following the fall of the Shah and started a war which lasted nearly a decade killing tens of thousands of Moslems and Christians alike. (there are many Christians living in Iran) Then he turned on the Kurds to the north with chemical weapons, then the marsh Arabs to the south, then as if this were not enough for good measure it was the turn of the Kuwaitis out of sheer greed. Each time the killing continued.

This is the lesson of history. The oil was important in the equation as despite sanctions it enabled Iraq each time to successively rearm for the next brutal incursion.

So we fly the flag out of respect for our armed forces and the job they are doing, it is not about winning or losing it is about thankfulness in the removal of a tyrant. Our best wishes to all who now attempt to rebuild democracy in this region.

26th April
Build up to Easter
A wonderful sparkling week this has been, with the sun shining, bright spring flowers everywhere and weeds still asleep in the gardens. Good to see spadework

going apace in the town's allotments down Cockstubbles and back of Alexandra Crescent – you can't beat a bit of fresh veg. when it comes right but I'm no expert.

The right start for Easter was the 'Easter Bonnet' competition on Maundy Thursday down at the Community Centre, thanks to fine efforts by Davina Clowes, Charlotte Harvey, Janet Woodward and a top hat number by James Clark. The centre has now been run by volunteers for the past year and a great job they are making of it – Debbie Clark, Wendy Wilson and Pat Kavanagh are the main team now with Maurice Smithard (he's been counting numbers for as long as anyone can remember down there) together with Anne, Vera Lawton and the Tranters. Well done team.

Help from outside /Assistance from Local Authorities

20th November
Borough Council Back-up for Uttoxeter Plus
Of course most of us were disappointed to hear that Peter Ross our Uttoxeter Plus Manager has now left us. However we are getting very good co-operation from the Borough Council in obtaining a replacement, hopefully to be in place not long after Christmas. It is so important to maintain momentum here. Now outline planning has been passed for the cattle market site (together with some very much wanted traffic improvements) we need to ensure that any improvements to the 70 existing retail outlets in the High Street and the Maltings can be properly promoted at the same time. When the new retail outlet is built we shall need to encourage shoppers to come from there through the archway into the town centre.

20th November
Public Toilets
Following a number of queries I reported at Town Council this week the progress on our new attended toilets on Bradley Street. We all welcome these, you recall planning permission was granted 12 months ago and I understood previously that work was scheduled to start earlier during the summer.

Although I was disappointed to hear of the decision made this week not to start work until after Christmas complete is scheduled by mid-April. Opening hours of these attended units would be 12 hours per day probably 7 am to 7 pm. We need to further discuss the need to retain the toilets on the other side of the maltings car park for use after 7 pm. I am sure we would like to hear readers views on this. At least we shall have facilities as usual for ALL our Christmas shoppers!

20th November
Pennycroft Park

There is no place in town that needs revamping more than Pennycroft Community Park and much consultation went on before the work recently started on the new footpaths. The present initiative will include better facilities for toddlers (you notice that the old play equipment has now been removed), a new separate junior play area for the 7 – 12 year olds to enable small children to play safely, a teenage multi-games area with tarmac playing surface with football goal and basketball hoop plus teenage shelter and skate board area.

That is the programme. I understand from Borough Council Community Services there is a 10 week contract on-going for completion by 16th December. I am not too happy on progress to date however, unfortunately outside contracts such as this if they fall behind at this time of year slip into the bad weather period – so watch this space!

At a later date two improved football pitches are proposed following application for finance to the Football Foundation – this is so important as I believe these are now the only 'municipal' pitches in the town.

28th November
Our Local Plan

Attending a planning training course at the Borough Council the other week reminded me of my growing unease with the delays to our new Local Plan said to be due to changes in the planning rules and 'directives from above.' Much of the consultation has been completed but now apparently the rules have been changed.

Of course these changes are to be welcomed bringing greater emphasis on the environment, the pre-assessment of projects for sustainability, getting quality and the essential use of brown field sites – but enough is enough, time is passing. The old Local Plan has now been out of date these past 47 weeks with no replacement in sight.

I strongly believe there is no substitute for site-specific information – local information based on national principles, amended as necessary according to local issues to inform us all (as well as the developers) what the changes to our local scene are likely to be. We need both the new Local Plan and individual site development plans in the cases where more advice is required.

My fear is that progress on all of this will be put on the shelf once we all get into political mode prior to the local elections in late April.

30th November
Our next local elections
Over the years of course our way of life in Uttoxeter has changed. Especially since the 80's people work longer hours – on the roads at 7.30 in the morning it used to be quiet with only a few fishermen venturing out to test the water, now they are full of white vans with lads with their trade tools in the back or else speeding career ladies off to earn a buck or two.

So when it comes to voting in elections we need as councils to remove as many restraints as possible in order to make voting easier for those working on shifts or away from home, for those who work long hours whether in the home or elsewhere, and for those who are disabled or who cannot get to the polling stations for whatever reason.

At the last general elections the Borough issued 82,000 postal votes to all those who asked for them. To carry on the trend they have applied this time for a 100% postal vote for the Borough and Town/parish elections scheduled for the end of next April. The outcome of the application will depend on what response they get and final ratification by the council. The Borough would do the job

POLLING STATION

NEW IDEAS, MORE VOTERS, MORE LOCAL DEMOCRACY.

WILLIE TRUELOVE ~ BASIC INSTINCT
RACHAEL M°SQUIRREL ~ GREEN
DICKY TRICKEY ~ FREE TRADE
CHARLIE FLATULANCE ~ WIND ENERGY

MORE OF A BUZZ OUT OF YOUR VOTE THESE DAYS GLADYS.

under the auspices of the Electoral Reform Society and they would do a fair check against fraud. The whole object would be to get the percentage of people voting up to the 40/50% region so the result is based on a fair range of opinion. I guess the future is with voting via the e-mail with an option for a postal vote but up to now the only method that has proved to increase the percentage turnout of electors is 100% postal.

25th January
Town Council Finance
This week in Council we have been sorting out the town's precept which is the cost to the ratepayer of running those things for which the Town Council is responsible, mainly the Town Hall facilities, the Heritage centre and the cemetery. Although this only amounts to 4.5% of your total Uttoxeter Council Tax we need to send the right message to the Borough and the County Councils.

This time we have been faced with estimates of the cost of dealing with the new cemetery safety regulations together with some disappointing income figures from the Town Hall. As a result we have been obliged to raise our part by 8.5% (annual cost per household £3.78) while retaining our recommended level of reserves at £27,000. Our Town Hall which was designed to handle the facilities for the old Urban District Council remains 25% empty despite part-occupation by Uttoxeter Plus. Our next priority therefore is to look with our partners at a one stop shop or other alternatives to bring the building into better use. We have open minds about how this can be done but the present position is unacceptable.

25th January
Public Toilets
You will be glad to see the old Bradley Street toilets being demolished in favour of new attended facilities open 12 hours per day. The thinking will be to provide agreeable facilities during the day for shoppers including children and babies. At nightime alternatives are available elsewhere – bearing in mind most of the complaints we have had with the present facilities are due to loutish behaviour at quiet periods and out of normal hours.

25th January
Pennycroft Park
Works to Pennycroft Park are also progressing well. The 'arena' for the older ones is complete and is already being used, the soft surface to the toddler play area

for the very young ones is being completed and the surface for the intermediate children's play area is being installed. I had some doubts about this but have been advised that it consists of a 2M wide flexible rubber lattice through which grass is allowed to grow. I looked at the first section as it was laid and this appeared very suitable.

25th January
Regional Assemblies

A referendum has been promised to decide on Regional Assemblies, in our case for the West Midlands. I believe the idea is to have a series of votes in different parts of the country at different times which seems a strange form of approach to me. Then we are told that these Regional Assemblies will take the place of County Councils, and District and Borough Councils will be replaced by Unitary Authorities. OK so far except for fear about escalating costs but I believe in principle that all Local Government needs a shake-up as often as practicable! So despite many fears that it would end up with the same people in different more expensive offices pushing around yet more paper without any commercial restrictions on finance it might do some good – but here is where I draw a clear line for 'thanks but please no more.' Why should this be so?

The reason is this; the guys who are behind all this do not care too much about improving our system of local government at all – they are Europeans wanting to divide up this country into manageable chunks of Regional Assemblies reporting direct to Brussels thereby bypassing our parliament! From the lesson of history, this I cannot and will never tolerate

1st February
Uttoxeter Plus

Those involved with Uttoxeter Plus and others also have been working hard this week to clear the first projects to be included in the next stage of the town's regeneration programme. I shall try to report on just where we have reached up to now.

It is now time we had a follow up to last year's works to the High Street. The new top surface to the roadway will soon be due and I am pleased to hear that retracting bollards are now being considered. These would prevent all vehicles travelling along the High Street during the daytime between the specified times. (I would suggest between the entrance to the Maltings shopping centre and Carter Street) This simple move would allow relaxed, safe shopping and various kinds of street selling noting that emergency vehicles will have the facility to drop the bollards to allow access at any time. Simple moves like this do seem to take time!

On Monday we had a presentation by Handforth Royal on their ideas for the High Street. This was the last part of the original Uttoxeter Plus Heath Check and first ideas towards our new Master Plan for the town centre. There certainly is much to do!

Quite rightly they emphasised that more attention was needed to detail. For example they suggested street furniture needed to be brought together in design with a common theme, from seats, litter bins and street lighting to tubs for flower planting. They noted the lack of trees particularly along the High Street and in the Maltings car park. Then they raised the big question of extending the walking areas from the High Street into the Market Place and showed illustrations of how this would look. This almost went back to the old days when the wednesday market stretched right from Bear Hill to the Old Talbot! Nowadays to avoid traffic gridlock this would need to be part of an overall traffic scheme. They also raised the question of restrictions to shop front colours but we felt that if the conditions were right this would follow on a voluntary basis. Altogether a taste of what needs to come forward as part of the Town Centre Master Plan.

Then we had the first appraisal team meeting for Uttoxeter Plus projects. You will be pleased to hear that the project brief prepared in conjunction with Borough Council for our Town Centre Master Plan was approved. Benefits (according to the wretched jargon of today) will be 'to encourage footfall in Uttoxeter Town Centre by simultaneously creating new opportunities for activity and attractions within the area, to improve community safety for pedestrians and to improve the connectivity of the town centre.' The most important purpose of all this will be to provide design guidance for the Borough Council and other stakeholders for regeneration works and to attract new investment into the town.

Also approved pending ratification of Advantage West Midlands was a £50,000 grant towards stimulating Uttoxeter businesses – an exciting new initiative. Attending this meeting was our interim Project Manager Alf Smith and our new Project Manager Elaine Burgess. She is already getting into the swing of things before commencing her duties in March.

Our problem is that we have no site specific planning guidance for the next stage of the town's development which surely must include not only the old cattle market and possibly the new cattle market, the High Street, the bus station and the train station! The sooner we have this guidance in our hands the better for all concerned.

15th February
Safer Routes to Schools
At the Safer Routes to Schools meeting earlier this week I was also concerned to hear that the vacancy for a school crossing person for the junction Stone Road/Stafford Road (mornings and afternoons) had not yet been filled. Seeing children safely across to school is such an important task – any volunteers please contact Pauline Allen, Education Department, Staffordshire County Council tel. 01785 27885

9th March
Regional Assemblies
You will be glad to know our doubts on Regional Assemblies were echoed last monday at the Borough Council who were unanimous in rejecting the idea of a local referendum just now. No-one wants our parliament bypassed. Our system of government has worked over the centuries through many a crisis far worse than that of today – coming together in the EU is fine for mutual benefit on all kinds of things but we need to watch out for this sort of hidden agenda.

26th April
All-Postal Elections
One thing about these all-postal elections which slightly concerns me is the matter of intrusion. Their purpose is to solely to increase the turnout and I have no problem with this. However they go on for around two weeks longer by the time it takes for the post and the Electoral Reform Society to do their bits and to return the ballot papers back (now all going to Burton to be counted). Every candidate has the democratic right to canvass for votes and if they wish to knock on doors to discuss matters with the public it is up to them. However to avoid intrusion the original plan was that the Electoral Reform Society would send by electronic mail to whoever asks, details of those who had voted to avoid unnecessary disturbance to those who had voted, especially during the Easter holidays but this has not been done. This means that people can be legally disturbed by a knock on the door up to 16 days after they have officially voted. I personally value our voting system above all else and do not wish the public to be put to any unnecessary inconvenience.

26th April
The war in Iraq
Praise to all who have brought the main shooting war in Iraq to initial conclusion.

Not only will it bring some kind of freedom to the country (in doing so it may split the country apart we don't know) but it will reinforce the message that oil riches should be used to promote democracy for the benefit of all.

3rd May
Postal Votes

All is quiet this week in council as away in the bowels of the Electoral Reform Society they are sorting out our postal votes and putting them into bundles of 100 ready for sending to the count. No polling stations, no fuss about notices, no days off school (sorry Tynsel Parkes staff and children). Let's face it less of that special feeling of achievement you get having dropped in your vote at 7.30 a. m. before going off to work or the feeling of support for our older folks just determined to get there to vote despite disabilities of all kinds. All for the worthy cause of increasing turnout but with more postal votes we do lose some of the special spirit and atmosphere of the polling booth.

Of course we get this only every four years and the new pilot voting system in East Staffordshire is an attempt to change old ways. In my view what we need most to bring things up to date is to attract younger people as councillors and this we shall only do if we take a much more flexible view on the four year period. Young people with or without families simply cannot these days make a commitment for this length of time and their views directly heard are so valuable.

Chapter 6

PROUD TO BE MAYOR OF EAST STAFFORDSHIRE

When I was kindly asked if I would like to be a Mayor of the Borough of East Staffordshire (which included Burton, Uttoxeter, Tutbury and the villages in between) I never thought to enquire if this involved some kind of traditional forfeit on the lines suffered in the old days by the young coopers of Burton; a good tarring, feathering and barrel roll following anointment by a jug of Marstons Pedigree. Alternatively for an oldie it might be: after four pints in the Coopers Tavern to recite by heart the names of 40 of the 47 original breweries in Burton, followed by the trick question and this was the killer punch (no conferring) – the position and prominence of the nearest 20 of the 47 level crossings, all long since disappeared. I suppose I was not disappointed to find no such forfeits existed, just a traditional inauguration with lots of friends shaking hands wishing us well.

We were now faced with a year of enjoyable engagements which, although we did not know it at the time, would be numbered over 300. Fortunately we were provided with a chauffeur and the mayoral car which took us between engagements in good comfort, the driver's job being to deliver us to our destination in what could be described as a relaxed and confident mood. I must say with the state of the traffic and before the days of 'sat. navs' this was not always the case, however provided we were prepared to stick in a layby for up to 20 minutes in some cases to ensure we got there on time the system worked but this sometimes produced some curious looks from passers-by who definitely queried our intentions!

The principle was always to attend functions within East Staffordshire as a priority. For this reason the text is confined to comments on notable people and events that occurred strictly within the Borough of East Staffordshire. Names are generally omitted unless they refer to genuinely unpaid volunteers! At the same time, I have tried to show how what we do today is nearly always built upon the unique history of the town of Burton linked as it is with brewing and the adjacent centres of agriculture in the countryside within the remainder of the Borough.

Surprising Links with the Breweries and Local Water Companies

Would you believe even in these hallowed halls the connection with water recovery and good old-fashioned sewage continued. I really could not believe this – thinking that these matters were well in the past. Nevertheless after years at the sharp end it is true I was about to thoroughly enjoy something different being mayor after ten years away from the town and its breweries. But just what could this connection be?

It went back as far as the days of the first Mayor of the Borough of Burton William Henry Worthington in 1878. The next two mayors also having good brewing names (the second being Alsop and the third Evershed) set the ball properly rolling.

The old Coopers Tavern is a memory from the past not forgotten. It still stands as you may know as an Irish pub featuring a proper gas meter, the odd shamrock and on the ceiling a proper (not painted on) patina of cigar smoke keeping company with the cobwebs of the same vintage. In the old days when brewers held the purse strings they would close the door, exclude you and I, then sit around the barrel seat and do their deals ending with a handshake; those were the days. Back during the late 70s when we were trying to sell a brewery to the Iranians, yes the Iranians, who being mostly Shi-ites did take alcohol. When they came over to see us they were simply fascinated by the place, with the barrels on the stillage and the famous 'sophisticated' dispense system consisting of just a tap giving that special Burton glass of ale. When the barrel had quietened the glass was filled up to the top with no head, at least you got the most every time, otherwise it was often a jug to take home.

Thirty years later as mayor I left them a citation in tribute for having kept the place like a proper 'public house'; rightly part of the heritage of old Burton. Sadly the place still is not even listed, please don't chop it about.

Consequently, back in those days both fresh clean water and sewage disposal were very much the responsibility of the town. There was no Seven Trent technical back-up and the buck stopped strictly with the local team. They did their best which consisted of spraying the semi-treated sewage onto the local fields as a fertiliser. I had been to Clay Mills (Burton sewage or recovery works) for various reasons over the years, mainly in connection with quality control on a delightful little number very close to Sudbury Hall off the A38. It had to be cunningly hidden and smell protected in that position otherwise the average visitor to the Museum of Childhood would be most unimpressed, but that is another story. Now I could hardly believe it when on 29th August we were being officially invited to Clay Mills not to the existing treatment plant but to visit the pumping station which in the old days did the pumping across the fields to what everyone called the sewage farm. Our duties were firmly fixed. I was allowed to officially start the first recently refurbished old beam engine under very strict supervision which I certainly needed. The mayoress was to sound the whistle without supervision which surely she would not need. Steam for the job being supplied from one of the hand fed boilers going for the day. This was thanks to an 'out of sight out of mind, salt of the earth' character heaving the spade lifting coal by hand up over his head into a bunker in the boiler house next door. The job now being officially done, perhaps it could be said our very last act for the water and sewage had now been officially completed!

There was still the brewing side, in order to bring us up to date, we were pleased to except an invitation from two of my previous colleagues Bruce Wilkinson and Jeff Mumford to tour the Burton Bridge Microbrewery on the 8th March. This operation had incredibly survived against all odds due to their efforts for the past 25 years or so. Well done to them. It is sobering to think they had survived the old Burton names like Basses, Worthington, Allied Breweries, Ind Coupe, Trumans and Marstons (still going at least but in the hands of others). The tour was most interesting, in many ways they showed the way in the use of perfectly good second hand plant, Marstons new brewhouse please note!

Burton Town Hall, Insignias and Entertaining Visitors

There is no doubt at all that Burton has the great advantage of a superb British Traditional Town Hall having its roots in the old Liberal club. Especially of note is a remarkable blend of 19th century steelwork, brickwork, local tiling together with beautifully original carved stonework.

Other features are a beautiful oriole window at the far end of the Main Hall and at the stage end the famous Wurlitzer organ. I could never resist whilst admiring this room comparing its proportions for some reason with those of St Pancras Station without the railway lines!

From the mayor's parlour sometimes the sound of the Wurlitzer could be heard. I remember once going down to see who was playing and being surprised to find the catchy music was coming from a young boy around 13 years old accompanied by his parents. What a joy he was bringing to all who were listening to those special trembling notes we all associate with our well maintained, genuine (adjust with a screwdriver and a hammer not a touch pad) theatre organ. We often showed children that spot near the roof just outside the parlour where if you look carefully three faces are carved spookily together with (if you count) only five eyes.

We were pleased to host 'insignia' events about once a fortnight. Interesting features of the Council Chamber were explained; for instance some of those coats of arms on the windows of the council chamber on close inspection seem somewhat strange. Basically the first mayors had their own coats of arms which they proudly displayed but later mayors, not aspiring to such things, took the opportunity to make them up for themselves clearly the College of Heralds were not involved. Sometimes so it is said the heraldry work was done on the kitchen table. However I believe they made a good job, refreshing and great fun is to be had explaining the various thoughts behind the inclusion of Burton Albion colours, a crest of cricket wickets, a raptor for Leighton Buzzard, and an old fashioned (no way at all of avoiding the stings type) bee hive from an apiarist. Unfortunately we cannot afford such things these days but a competition for cubs or brownies to make up their own coats of arms well started by Cllr Dawn the previous mayor became most popular amongst young visitors. Then there are the flags of the nuclear submarines and the connection with the sinking of the 'Sharnhorst' in World War 2. Of course out of politeness we tended to cut this bit out from the itinerary when we entertained German visitors although it was a long time ago and almost forgotten. The Italian roof was also well worth a mention together with the erection of one of the first 'no smoking' signs early last century following a very expensive clean to remove the products of cigar smoking. Then there is the clock with a remote pendulum modified so they say to stop the seconds tick promoting sleep during long council meetings.

For instance on the 16th of June we were pleased to entertain the 23rd Brookhouse Brownies, much appreciated by the Vicky Shilton the Brownie leader, on the 12th August members of the Royal British Legion with Ken Compton their chairman, and after Coors Gardening Club, Burton 'Phab' club, A Plus and Stapenhill post-16 centre, on the 14th September we entertained 28 students and 3 staff from Gesamtschule Emsland who were visiting Abbot Beyne School as part of an ongoing exchange (without reference to German battleships). Then the Lions on 1st February followed by Age Concern on 9th March.

We also took the opportunity of hosting two 'at homes' on the 7th September and the 2nd November. These were held in the Council Chamber, Muniments Room and dining room for Borough residents from all walks of life. These were I believe much enjoyed, the rooms being packed with local people who almost without exception had never visited this part of the Town Hall before, tombola in aid of mayor's charities. We really wanted to emphasise, with the agreement of the Council of course, that these beautiful surroundings were the property of the borough and could be enjoyed by all who were prepared to treat them with proper respect.

15th October

Just in time for the summer holidays this was the year of the *amazing maize maze*; it amazed us anyway. It was all at Postern Farm, made ready for a day out for all on sunny days during summer holidays. They start at planting time with high tech transponders acting as an accurate first reference from which to mark out the theme of the year straight from the drawing board. Then they plant the maize strictly along the reference lines making complicated pathways – not forgetting emergency ways out for those who want to get home for supper, get out of the rain or possibly just want a comfort break.

When the maize grows tall you can't see the shape nor can you see people in the maze. So what can you do to contact them? Actually officially you can't but they can contact the management, as everyone is given a flag before entering which when held up can be seen from the 'goon tower' by the control centre, or I suppose you can just shout. Well done Postern Farm.

The World's First Air Show

The world's first air show was quite the most unexpected event connected with Burton, I had worked in the town for nearly 10 years and had never heard of it.

In the town people are generally quiet and modest about things, but one thing we need to be proud about in particular is the world's first air show known as the Aviation Week which took place between the 26th of September and the 1st October 1910 barely six years and 283 days since Wilbur and Orville Wright first took off in a heavier than air craft from the beach at Kitty Hawk.

No less than seven aviators took part on this truly auspicious occasion time from the wetlands down by the Trent in Burton.

The official entry price was 5/- (five shillings) including a programme with an additional charge of 2/6 (two and six) to visit the hangers. Incredibly one of the pilots was a woman and there are few of them in the business 95 years later! The brave lady who took part was Mademoiselle Elaine Dutrieu who flew a Farman biplane and thankfully came to no harm.

Notable were the Bleriot planes having recently flown the channel. Burton was certainly on the map of history that week, no serious accidents were recorded although a number failed to reach their destinations – some said after flying on a set course they landed in a fair spread between Basses water tower and Lichfield.

Of particular interest also were a number powered by the 50 hp Gnome rotary engine which like a number of later engines during the First World War sported a static crankshaft around which the propellers and cylinders rotated. The arrangement was purely to save weight. Unfortunately with it also came a throttle having only two positions fully on and fully off! A one-way lubrication system which ending in a fine spray well dosed the pilot with castor oil, huge gyroscopic forces which made the planes difficult to turn left and overall danger-

ous to fly completed the picture.

The airshow had one lasting memorial. Mary Jenkins, the mayoress at the time, was presented with what is now the Borough Mayoress's evening chain by her husband the mayor, purchased from the proceeds of the Aviation Week. This is a most magnificent piece of jewellery which has in the very centre an enamelled depiction of one of the aircraft flown on that most memorable of occasions. When worn even now the mayoress becomes the envy of everyone in sight, whoever they may be.

1211 Squadron Air Cadets includes some young people from Burton so we were very pleased to attend. The air training Corps play a big part in recruiting for the RAF. I was impressed by the standard achieved by the cadets. Having done some solo flying myself as a cadet I was also singularly unimpressed by my performance on the flight simulator having achieved a theoretical landing deep in the next parish but one. Thank goodness this flying business is now in the hands of the younger generation.

Not forgetting we have these intrepid flyers from 1910 to thank as we confidently climb the steps of our jumbo en route for yet another exotic foreign holiday.

National Waterways Canal Festival, Art is Rubbish and
20th Annual Gathering of Greyhound Boat Club

During the year we had the very good fortune of hosting the National waterways Festival held in Burton at Shobnall fields down by the Trent and Mersey Canal. Like much good fortune this had come to us by accident, the venue previously agreed having fallen through.

Our starter before the event was 'Art is Rubbish.' on 7th July, children from various first schools were asked to create their impressions of the effects of disposal of rubbish in our waterways. It certainly made everyone think and brought together Stretton Brook, Grange Community School, Belvedere School, Violet Lane infants, William Shrewsbury School, Crown Special School, Funshine after School Club, and Shobnall primary school. This was sponsored by the Inland Waterways Association and Recycle East Staffordshire. We had a get-together afterwards when prizes were awarded and the youngsters encouraged to briefly talk about their exhibits.

About this time it was confirmed by the organisers that the Festival was expected to attract around 30,000 people over three days with around 300 narrowboats moored for several miles along the canal towards Marstons Brewery. I will admit to a slight panic here but to their credit the council team held firm and anyway the organisers handled this kind of thing every year, confidence fairly oozed out of them.

I do believe the view of Marston's traditional Burton brewery right alongside the canal, well complimented by the smell of hops and a whisper of steam from the brewhouse and all surrounded with a huge pile of traditional wooden barrels gave the edge to Burton when the festival organisers became anxious to fix the alternative venue.

Up to this time neither the mayoress nor I had experienced the joy of the trip on a canal boat or experienced the possible perils of so doing. Happily the first thing the organisers did was to take us up the Trent and Mersey to show us what it is like. We thoroughly enjoyed it all so relaxing but I did find when steering the boat (when they offered) to be somewhat soporific, inevitably emerging out of one's reverie heading directly for the bank and trouble.

Once the site was agreed we attended meetings of the organisers. These became more and more exciting and professional as time went on. The Council were also positive in encouraging other events to take place at the same time via the Town Centre Management, they had for instance organised a successful Flower Festival in St Modwen's church on these dates.

Back to Shobnall where each member of their team had been given a specific responsibility which in most cases was well known from the previous year. Nevertheless we were amazed when questions were asked like – how is the dredging going on? Progress with the piling? Moorings organised? – in each case the answer came back in the positive from someone who clearly knew what they were doing! Then an articulated lorry appeared on site containing all the little things people go crazy wanting just before an event like this, connections for water, facilities for security, 300 mooring fixtures, items to improving access, special nuts and bolts and so on; all in the capable hands of Mr fix-it.

As the great day approached the punters began to arrive. Some by boat from the south having taken six weeks or so travelling began to take up the moorings. Then five days before the event it began to rain and rain …

I thought our best ploy was to call in every evening after our engagements to try to give them a morale boost but this always ended up the other way – they were OK how are you and how about a pizza?

This is where import from the professionals paid off. They cancelled the heavy exhibits to prevent the showground becoming a quagmire from which they could not possibly recover in time. This effectively kept the state of site under control, acceptable to the public and reduced remedial work afterwards.

About this time the council were faced with the problem of gypsies who came in out of the woodwork (as they do). We had arranged for a temporary car park to be provided in a field not far from the brewery. The field had been secured against intruders by means of an earth ramp effectively keeping out all unwanted guests. Seeing their opportunity the gypsies had lined up their vehicles outside the field ready to enter just as soon as we removed the earth barrier to let in the public. Most unusually for a council and thanks to some very forward thinking by staff we were able to get one step ahead of them by arranging car parking (that was for around 500 cars) at a derelict site nearer to the centre of town. We then delayed erecting notices until the night before leaving our unwanted guests left parked outside an empty field still protected by the earth ramp! I may have been wrong but I did believe their intentions far exceeded what was involved in just attending the event.

We were to perform the official opening and thankfully the weather improved for the day. Beforehand however we were to meet the mayor of Halton who would be presiding over the festival next year scheduled to take place at Preston Brook. Just before he was to arrive we heard of all things that he was in gaol! Of course all in public life do take a certain risk in this direction but we did consider this one to be a little over the top. However the tale proved totally groundless and he turned out to be a most respectable gentleman with a charming wife. They both enjoyed their visit and all was well and so we were ready to perform the opening ceremony. This was to be done by us travelling from Horninglow Basin to the festival site in a very special narrow boat called *The President*. This really was special being the only narrow boat out of two presently existing powered by steam.

So there we were – the mayoress and myself plus some expert boaters and a stoker. *The President* had steam up, engine going and whistling merrily, and at the same time we were being entertained by a four piece band playing traditional instruments all ready and on time for the job in hand. That is until we tried to pass through the Horninglow exit lock when *The President* ground to a halt, stuck on the sill of the lock. My uninitiated thoughts were that being steam powered and having a boiler presumably made the boat travel lower in the water.

At this stage I was for panicking and running away across the fields but once again such thoughts were stopped in their tracks by the experts advising that some advantage could be gained by waiting for the lock to fill up a little more. This effectively also gave *The President* time to raise full steam pressure and with safety valve blowing and pistons hammering away at full speed we passed over the sill and panic over!

In the end despite the weather we did get around 30,000 people attending over three days and were pleasantly surprised to find how local residents accepted all these visitors with very good grace. The first question invariably being 'where is the nearest pub' easy to answer this but then the locals were offering to do washing and to supply their various needs everyone ended up happy. As to what their various needs were I did not feel it was my duty in any way to enquire. The whole event went very successfully and on the Sunday we were privileged to receive a visit from Timothy West and Prunella Scales. They were there to receive their 'Waterway Personality of the Year' awards from Canal and River Rescue during the closing ceremony.

Later on the 12th of November at our Civic Ball we were honoured by the presence of Mr John Fletcher the National Chairman of the Inland Waterways Association who kindly proposed the toast to the Mayor.

As if the National Festival were not enough we also attended the annual Greyhound Boat Club gathering at Horninglow Basin on 18th September. We were pleased to see what local clubs can do on their own, once again this was a great day for boat owners and for local families alike. There was a good attendance. We then had the onerous task of judging the best decorated boat which we survived after taking some quietly spoken advice. Notable was their object of the Greyhound Boat Club – 'drawing attention to the Trent & Mersey Canal and giving a bit of colour to this part of Burton,' over the years they are gradually succeeding

You can't win them all
Whether you are Mayor or anything else you can't win them all.

This became all too obvious for the mayor and the solo carol singer during the Christmas lights switch on. We had travelled to the dais in the marketplace without difficulty in a fine vintage motor car and were soon surrounded by a crowd of parents with small children, mostly carried on the shoulder ready for the switch on. Soon the area around the dais was packed.

First the lady carol singer had difficulties with the microphone. When the time came for the mayor to say a few words, just to thank everyone for coming, to recognize the efforts made by those who had erected the lights and those who had prepared the firework display (a very few words but appropriate) it was time for the microphone and amplifiers to exhibit yet again their capacity to cause confusion, this time transforming the mayors English into what some African ex-pats. might describe as an obscure but intermittent version of Swahili. Not to worry, the fireworks were a great success.

Visit of Jean Claude Van Damme
Either you are into these kinds of movies or your not. When I heard that the great man was visiting the area and causing a great deal of commotion in anticipation, I frankly had never heard of him. Quite clearly the girls in the office had, he must have been special but when they offered to replace John the driver for that morning he must be very special! My thoughts ran to a rally driver of the 1950's, but that was Sheila Van Damme, about 80 by now I should say, there surely could be no connection and why, if he was an international film star, did he choose to visit us here just across the river from little old Burton on Trent? He was billed to go to the Bretby Centre just over the river to the old Mining Research Centre now converted with conference and other facilities.

Enquiries were made and it turned out he was to come by kind invitation of the local karate club in Burton direct from London as part of his UK tour. (they had done extremely well to organise this). He duly came in a convoy of two Land Rovers direct from London and was instantly recognisable by his dark glasses and extremely confident manner. Whilst he was taken up the stairs with his entourage to freshen up I, amongst a crowd of others, waited for him just along the corridor whilst around 100 local karate enthusiasts waited downstairs in karate kit for a teach-in. He was even spied at as he left the loo, that's the price of fame I suppose, anyway he talked around and I had a fairly long conversation with him to the extent that I thought it really was about time he gave his demo. He seemed a nice ordinary guy as I welcomed him and we spoke of his family and so on but as he later went through his routine he did seem very special as he gave I would say more of a 'control in life' experience. It was rather over the top for many young boys and girls there around the age of nine or ten whose parents had paid a very large sum (at least I so I was told) for being present. At the appointed time back to the cars and off for two more appearances that day and that was it.

He gave me his picture which was notable in that he refers to me as 'Lord Mayor of Burton,' This reminded me strangely of the old days when the real Lord Burton was seriously developing St Paul's Square including the Town Hall, which he had moved from the Market Place, as a claim for city status (which brings with it the title of Lord Mayor). I very much doubt if history will be repeated, overall most people enjoyed his visit, good luck to him, henceforth for us he will be strictly on the telly.

Visit to Toyota motor Manufacturing (UK) Ltd, Burnaston

This visit was important to us, as although the works are in Derbyshire, Toyota is a major employer also in East Staffs. We thanked South Derbyshire district Council for this opportunity. Firstly we had a slight disappointment, our mayoral car – unique in this area – was at that time a Toyota Lexus. However this had no recognition at these works as all Lexus cars are built in Japan. The main production at Burnaston being the Corolla.

Unimportant things aside however, this is a tough time for car manufacture in the UK particularly with plants in Birmingham closing and doubts on the future of Jaguar. My lasting impression of this plant however is of a dedicated workforce, well-paid, well organised, and getting on with the job. The various parts are received at one end of the factory, and arranged individually before being fed onto the track which moved with very little interruption. Assembly by teamwork was very evident with no one hanging around. I am not normally impressed by manufacturer's buzz-words, but when they talk about 'motivated people who are treated with respect will show great commitment to the fulfilment of the company's objectives' I believe they mean it. We were taken round the production lines in the tour train which gave us an uninterrupted view of the operation so little could be hidden. My view is that all things being equal Toyota is well able to fend off competition in the UK, its cars are generally 'carbon friendly' with design moving in the right direction for the future.

Mayor and consort, May 2002 (p29)

Graham Coxon, Burton's famous macebearer

Pippa delivers his stuff (p31)

Conference amongst the gravestones! (p31)

Holes for granite planets (p32)

A proper armilliary sphere? (p33)

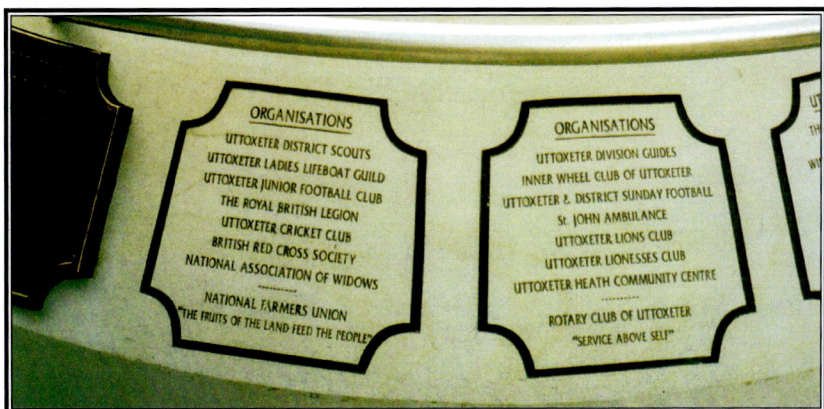

Plaques engraved any more spellings? (p33)

With the ladies Morris (p79)

With Dr Martin Kruze former arch. of Berlin and Bernard Grunberg (p84)

Heiner Pott, Mayor of Lingen with Franz Ratuscho from Ukraine (p84)

The Green Team from Picknalls (p87)

A cycle team, Arch. Nichols from Birmingham and Fr. McGinley, St Modwens, Burton (p94)

Saluting team, Town Hall steps (p72)

Past the Advertiser office (p72)

Burton's famous Wurlitzer organ (p74)

With John Fletcher, Chairman IWA (p77)

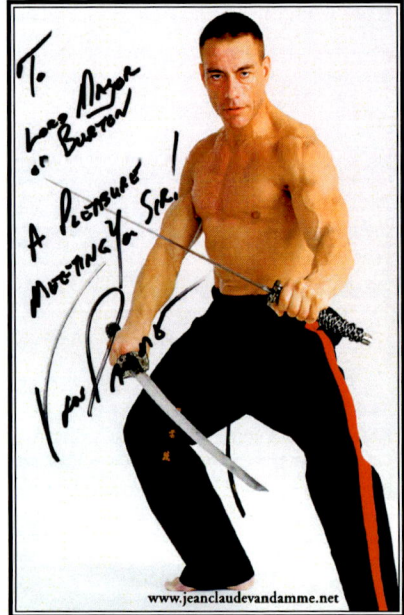

Jean Claude flattering - thank you sir! (p80)

Off with the team in the President (p79)

U X's rugby keep well out of the way! (p99)

Hockey lives on! (p102)

A fine turn out Burton Sea Cadets (p114)

Mayoress in sari - a warmer day! (p118)

I could not help having a small flashback (as old men do) to the time this site was Derby airport and I as a young cadet took the opportunity of 'pranging' a Miles Magister just about on the spot where the paint shop is now. I was not the most popular person at this time as, if I recall, I had recently also reversed the family car into our gatepost damaging both.

Burton College

It was our pleasure to host the Burton College Higher Education graduation ceremony in the town Hall. This ceremony was for no less than 276 students who had graduated in many subjects from BA(Hons) Business Management to HMD electrical engineering to HNC computing and so on.

We noted especially that the College has taken great steps to link the courses it offers with what is required by the community of Burton on Trent. As well as the normal intake it also offers top-up education for all those in the community who need fresh skills or who have previously left full-time or other education too early. In this respect we also attended their annual awards ceremony on 15th March where the various College Schools awarded their prizes for effort. Many local companies had made contributions towards these prizes in recognition of the service Burton College provides in terms of satisfying their requirements. The JCB project of the year was awarded to Timothy Guyatt and the Toyota Shield for Best Student in Engineering to Karl Staley.

We also attended the launch of their new computer bus. The bus with its computer facilities is to be used to outreach into companies and other organisations for training purposes.

The Constitutional Club

This account certainly would not be complete without mention of the Constitutional Club. Its very name invokes a dilemma, something about the digestive system and one's constitution in general spring to mind. To visit you go in directly off the High Street. Being almost next door to Basses offices. It is as if it had caught the same style with a mixture of dark oak, believed to be Spanish Mahogany, glass either stained in art nouveau style or what appears to be beautifully etched glass. Words like baroque scrolled wooden pediments, dentil moulding supports, fluted pilasters, 'linen fold' carvings for capitals on newel posts simply spring out of their official 'notes for volunteers;' rather like the script for an architects exam first class. A visit to the toilet is to be recommended and enjoyed for the exquisite doorway, the chequerboard tiles with lead piping leading to old fashioned taps in huge hand basins. This was the place where in the old days all sorts of brewing business was done – that is after it ceased being a Post Office. One can hardly believe how such a place with rooms for cards, a bar and billiard room, with poor access for parcels from the street, ever could be used as such, but it was. The mayor thanked the Constitutional Club for the use of the bowling green as used by the his bowling team (mostly fairly mediocre at bowls but major on the talk, enjoying the company and trying the beer) the regular quiz nights they put on for charity (once a year for the mayor's charity), and last but not least the Christmas pantomimes, much enjoyed in which the mayor (whose seat was always on the front row at the end) became a suitable target for small fire of all descriptions. Thank you.

Twinning celebration between East Staffs and Lingen, Raisdorf exchange visits for 60 years since liberation, 21 years of twinning and discontinuing Uttoxeter's twinning with Raisdorf.

Relations with Lingen continue to thrive after no less than 21 years! Quite remarkable to see this carry on undiminished, the Borough Council working in a supportive role with their friends in the Rathaus at Lingen; as it should be, allowing the many contacts built up over the years to continue and thrive.

There are many aspects of life in Germany during World War II of which we in this country are unaware.

As a result of our long-term friendship with the people of Lingen, we as a Borough were honoured to receive an invitation to attend their **commemoration of 60 years since their liberation** from the shackles of war by Capt. Ian Liddell VC with his team from the Coldstream Guards together and others on the 3rd April 1945.

I was pleased to accept this invitation on behalf of the Borough, and in this was well supported by Linda Smith (Head of the Borough Central Services as she was then). This was always to be an emotional visit and so it turned out. Lingen is on the edge of the flatlands not far from the Dutch border near Arnhem. It was notable in those days for its extensive railway yards. As the war progressed many Ukrainians had been imported as slave labour to replace the many young men who were away in the German army fighting. When the war ended the remnants were returned to Lingen and the Ukrainians similarly to their country, but this time only to be murdered by Stalin. War is a very cruel business.

The Lingen authorities had arranged a very appropriate event. Just by the Rathaus (Town Hall) there was an exhibition of pictures taken during 1945, including a famous one of the Coldstream Guards relaxing, in one of those rare moments when they were able, in the traditional way by enjoying a hot cuppa.

There was also a get-together in Lingen Theatre on the next day, the auditorium was packed. Local young people then gave their positive views for the future. When it was my turn I first expressed my thanks to be invited and confirmed the will of the people of Burton that our friendship should continue (in my very basic German made slightly less basic by kindly help from two council employees) which was well received.

It was an experience I shall always remember, however this is now well into the past and now we must be looking forward into the future as joint members of the EU and NATO. They had invited as chief guests the previous Archbishop of Berlin Dr. Martin Kruse a long time resident of Lingen now retired who was in office when the Berlin Wall came down, Bernard Grunberg, a representative from the Jewish community presently living in Derby and 'Franz' Ratuscho an Ukrainian, now well into his 80s, who was resident in Lingen during the war and who remarkably despite these terrible events has survived until now.

In Burton the 21 years celebration started with an official visit by a Lingen delegation who arrived on 8th July. Events began with an informal get-together to 'cement relations,' then a tour of Coors visitor centre, singing in the Octagon Centre and Burton Place with a celebration concert later in the town hall and further participation in Burton regatta on the 11th of July where the visiting Lingen rowers happily joined in the races.

But there was more, table tennis has always been a very popular sport, the Burton club including both international and county players celebrated its 20th anniversary the this year. Considering both their age and what they were up against, the visiting Lingen team gave a very good account of themselves against a full Burton team. Again later in the year as part of the celebrations during one week in October, the Burton and District Football Association hosted a guest team from S.V.Olympia near Lingen. Again very good time was had by all.

A most distasteful event occurred at Uttoxeter Town Council when the majority of Councillors voted to discontinue twinning relationships with Raisdorf. This had continued for a number of years and had done much to secure good relations between the two towns. However all is not lost. After receiving a message from Linda Macdiarmid of Thomas Alleynes School, Uttoxeter to the effect that a limited exchange was taking place this year, I was very pleased to take the students around Burton Town Hall which hopefully did something to repair relations without contravening what had been agreed.

Burton Civic Society

We attended the annual General meeting of the Civic Society. We were pleased to see how the Society continues to act on its responsibility to do their best to ensure good building works in the town. This is done by commenting on planning applications and recognizing best building works by means of plaques on chosen buildings, those for 2004 were presented during the meeting. They also aim to encourage general knowledge of the town by holding interesting talks at various intervals. We attended Richard Stones' talk on 3rd November on the book he has recently written on the town of Burton, this seemed a good read.

We were also pleased to attend a daffodil 'plant in' at Curtis Court on Horninglow Road on 24th October, it is good to see that despite our amateurish approach to this delicate job the bulbs still survive.

Relations with the Police Force

The mayor is non-political and as such I felt that it was the duty of the mayor to support initiatives by the police and as such following discussions with Chief Superintendent Smy we were pleased to accept his invitation to visit Burton Police Station on the 20th September. He explained the police now considered it was their duty to act not only to uphold the law but to act on the things of concern to the public like graffiti and antisocial behaviour of all types. This depended on local needs, and each locality was in some ways different; a new concept indeed. We then had the opportunity of going round the station and meeting as many staff as were available (even in the darkest corners) mainly to thank them for what they were doing as I don't suppose they have many thank-you social visits of this kind.

Like any police station suspected criminals are brought in at all hours and we were impressed by the sergeant (no names I'm afraid) whose job was to decide whether to lock the person up prior to questioning, for the sake of the public, or to let him or her free after a good talking to, (clip on the ear not allowed) to save money. I thought back to my time in the desert where we had a case of money being stolen on site. The man, finding the theft, was frightened what might happen to him, as standard practice was to deduct the sum from his wages, so he made the mistake of calling the police. They came, called for the residents of nearby cabins, rounded them up and took them to the station where they beat their feet to extract confessions. The situation was only resolved when their manager agreed to pay money for their release.

First schools and Head Teachers

Personally I can hardly remember the first school I attended at the age of five at Nuthall near Nottingham. My brother and I were later pushed off to a school in the city, and a few years later to another school at Loughborough. Then I was off to study engineering in 1959 in the smoke at Manchester.

My thoughts towards education for years after was focused almost entirely on life as a student, what had happened at school did not matter. I took pleasure out of obscure bits of mathematics and engineering which seemed the things that mattered to me, (would you believe) never forgetting the dread of being thrown out of the course. We were taught (if that is the right word) by a team of lecturers who were both obsessed by their own status and who in general cared little or nothing for the success of their students. Basically if 40% of students did not make to the end of the course then so what. There was no censure, it would be put down to a poor intake. After all applicants always well exceeded places.

They did not realise by failing a student, who could have passed if better taught, they were rejecting not only years spent as a student but the efforts made by teachers in all the schools which he or she had attended were to be largely thrown away. Added to which there was the stigma of failure which in those days almost invariably acted as a barrier to future progress.

Then the clouds lifted and I was fortunate to be presented with a super daughter in law who was a primary school teacher and at the same time I was almost obliged to take up the position as governor at a local first school.

Then my mistake became clear, I realised the most important part of schooling was getting the children off to a good start at their first school and carrying on the good work taking on board all the advances until it was time to leave school. By that time they could be better prepared for further education which is now presented in a much more caring and positive way.

So when it came to the mayoral duties I was very pleased to attend as many schools who were prepared to invite us. Sometimes first schools asked for mayoral robes to be worn, in which case I avoided taking the mace, somewhat against protocol, for safety reasons. One can only imagine the mayhem that it might be caused. So on these occasions it was left strictly back at the town hall or perhaps, if required later in the day, locked safely out of sight in the boot of the mayoral car.

I might say full mayoral robes were popular with younger children but sensibly I would not dare to appear like this with the older children on an informal basis. The fear of grown-up remarks of all kinds might tend to degrade the office.

One visit we must mention here was to a school at the top of the hill in Burton, many of you can guess where it was for it has now been 'reorganised.' The headmaster was also a councillor who (I think he would admit) used to adopt a slightly aggressive some would say dogmatic attitude in Council. However there was something about him which made me suspect in his day job he was totally professional and caring. Anyway there were so few councillors like him who, having a day job as well, were prepared to give up their time in the evenings for civic matters.

I'd tried a number of times to obtain an invitation to visit the school and finally by nefarious means (I won't go into this) he kindly invited us.

We duly attended the school and were pleased to join with the staff and children during their special assembly. The whole school had recently attended a residential course for one week and had much enjoyed the experience. Their schedule had included outdoor activities including some canoeing on the local lake which had been much enjoyed. We then joined them in some special songs they had learnt during the course, including if I remember some interesting body movements, after which the assembly duly ended.

The headteacher then kindly took us round the school, we said our goodbyes and walked across the playground towards the waiting mayoral car. It was playtime for the children and we were surprised when they all moved across and finally surrounded us – asking nicely about what it was like to be mayor, and whether we related to the Royal family and so on. Such was their politeness, good behaviour and honest straightforwardness I must say my knees went genuinely wobbly and I was glad on the one hand to reach the car and on the other so happy to have been there at last before reorganisation finally put an end to what had been clearly a happy school.

We also enjoyed visits to Belvedere Junior School; the onerous choice of best Easter egg in their competition just before Easter holidays fell to us and to their Festival of Harvest celebrations on the 20th of October. Well done.

Lifeboats in Burton?

In East Staffordshire we are about as far from the sea as you can get. After a roasting summer holiday spent by some of us on the golden sands of Torquay I suppose one can only imagine these places in the winter, lashed with storms, all hiked up by the TV pictures, not forgetting those wonderful books you open to read over the holiday, about lighthouse history, including mandatory gory details of death amongst the crew of three, the remaining two wondering about being tried for murder, trapped under the light waiting in vain for the rescue boat. Would you believe we have a cabinet in the mayor's rooms full of lifeboat plates as proof of the wonderful job done by local ladies over the years, collecting money for this very good cause. Let me say from experience that woe betide any mayor who dares to face a lifeboat dinner (following the request 'please say a few words Mr Mayor') without being fully prepared as to the facts of the latest self-righting lifeboat boat with the necessary details of where and when.

Chapter 7

OTHER SPECIAL EVENTS IN EAST STAFFORDSHIRE

Mayoral Service

One strange aspect of St Mary's Church Parish Church in Uttoxeter which I was prompted to comment upon during our Borough mayoral service is its clock tower. Not all the tower sides have a clock face and the parts of town where the clock face is directly visible to check the time are remarkably few, being almost confined to the first floor office of Northgate doctor's surgery and the very top end of the market place. Understandably even they were not prepared to supply the extra clock face, then wait 300 years for Tescos!

There is more however. Very much effort was made in those days to provide a carillon which can be heard four times per day based on the time shown on the clock face, a new popular tune every day. This is no podcast however, the choice of tunes was apparently based on what was available and further restricted to what could be played on the eight bells as re-hung in 1905. No-one has ever heard of Friday's tune so some people call it the Staffordshire tune and I've no idea where it came from. The sequence goes like this, surprisingly the only hymn tune is on Sunday.

Sunday	*O worship the king*
Monday	*Bright Shining Eyes*
Tuesday	*The last rose of summer*
Wednesday	*The Minstrel Boy*
Thursday	*Where has my Highland Laddie Gone?*
Friday	*The Staffordshire Tune*
Saturday	*Home sweet home*

One seriously wonders about Thursday's tune – could it really be true that this choice is referring to the Duke of Monmouth's surrender of his Scottish army in Uttoxeter and hence the end of the Civil War?

Burton Statutes Fair, Showmen's Guild

The statutes fair is a popular Burton tradition. Historically it was the event where farm labourers were set on to work by farmers for the following year.

Now it is just a matter of all the fun of the fair. It is so easy these days to find an excuse to cancel these traditional events for reasons ranging from traffic disruption to local shopkeepers complaining about reduced sales (most fairs increase sales despite some disruption) to the cost of policing. A good time is had by all but unfortunately those having a good time never feel the need to tell the council about it, so all that is heard by the council are complaints.

To try to get round this the Showman's Guild of Great Britain meet councillors at their splendid annual luncheon, this year on the 25th February at the Ramada Hotel, to put matters straight. Another of their legitimate gripes is that they get confused with gypsies. Gypsies are of all types but those who take sites over and leave piles of litter have become a real nuisance to the community. To confuse showmen who travel the country on strictly fixed programmes as they do within the Guild is unfair.

However, as Mayor I was happily required to open the fair with the steadying assistance of the Rev. Farthing. To achieve this we accordingly set ourselves down in a kind of bucket which quite obviously was set to perform some quite horrendous loops and descents. Whilst the press were taking their photographs

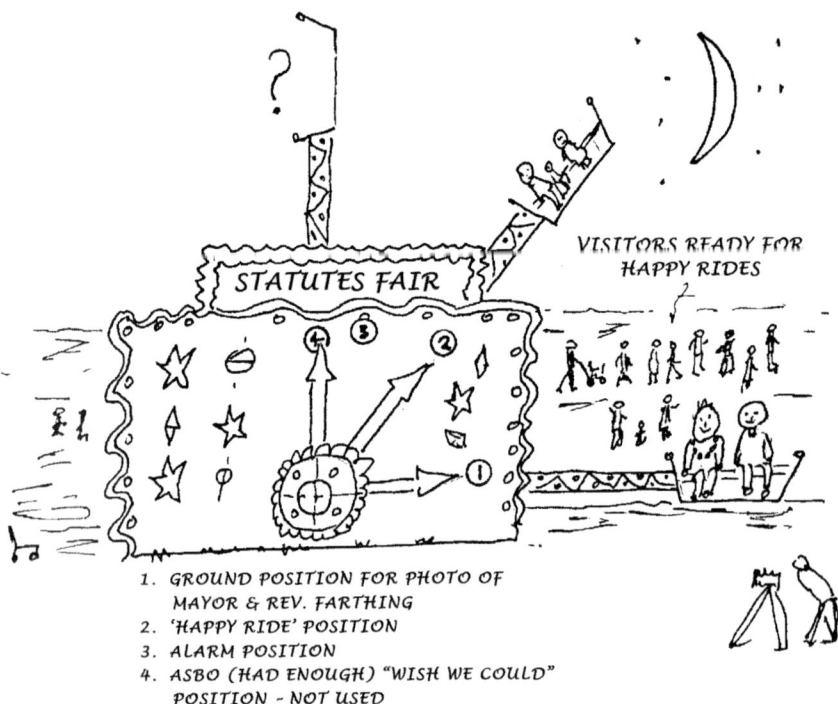

STATUTES FAIR

VISITORS READY FOR
HAPPY RIDES

1. GROUND POSITION FOR PHOTO OF
   MAYOR & REV. FARTHING
2. 'HAPPY RIDE' POSITION
3. ALARM POSITION
4. ASBO (HAD ENOUGH) "WISH WE COULD"
   POSITION - NOT USED

we took the opportunity to ensure that no one had paid any money to ride just yet and that there was consequently no chance of the ride starting up and destroying our dignity!

I was pleased to see that efforts were being made right across the Midlands by the showmen to keep these old fairs running. Mostly by presenting the true facts to various councils knowing that once fairs are stopped even for one year it is difficult if not impossible for them to be reinstated.

Concert Tutbury Castle

As there is little of the old castle structure left and no proper permanent facilities for such events, Tutbury Castle has always been a difficult venue to put on a successful event like 'The Land of Hope and Glory' concert held on a warm summer's evening in July. However Tutbury Castle Ltd well overcame all these difficulties. Various performers in high-quality fancy dress spiced up the evening and an orchestra and choir performed traditional music. This all made to create a splendid patriotic atmosphere. The event was very well attended, the hillside being full of people enjoying themselves. I include this event as I believe such occasions are so important to keep the name of Tutbury fully on the map for such high-class performances. Once again this was a case of a village working together and producing something rather special.

Rolleston on Dove Day of Traditional English Events

Rolleston Special Events Committee put on a Day of Traditional English Events. Various local people including the children had made a number of attractive boats out of cardboard and other materials which brightly painted were floated down the river by the church. These made a very attractive sight somewhat reminiscent of the Far East. Added to this knights were jousting, an exhibition of local paintings was going on in the nearby hall, teddy bears were travelling up on to the church roof and the church itself was open to various activities. Well done RODSEC for putting on something attractively different.

Marchington

I as delighted to be present when the trophy 'Best Kept Village' was presented to the Chairman of the Marchington Parish Council. I noted the trophy takes the form of a curious totem-pole-like obelisk which fits into a sizable hole in the ground which I did notice had hardly the time to fill itself in since they last won the trophy. Well done Marchington.

Burton and District Model Boat Club, Burton Conservation Volunteers, a hill in Stanton, Refurbished hall in Newchurch

We were pleased to 'hit the water' at Branston Water Park to witness the activities of the Burton and District Model Boat Club, all model boat enthusiasts. They have been going for no less than 25 years with scale boats, yachting, fast racing boats and static models. They have a freshly tarmaced slipway and first class facilities. Only sorry we could not stay longer, the Water Park is a perfect venue.

We also took the opportunity the following month of having Lawrence Oates, as ever in 'shorts' order, show us the work the Burton Conservation Volunteers are doing installing matting, dropping gabions, installing temporary fencing and setting seeds and plugs, and generally uprating the banks for the enjoyment of visitors and to better hold the soil which will lead to wild life improvement.

The next two events took place in what is truly deepest East Staffordshire. the first was at Stanton not far from Croxton on the top of a rather slippery hillside way out in the country. A set of unique glass stones to be set in a dry stone wall was the brainchild of artist Jenny Blant. We are proud to say that, despite some rather inappropriate footwear the mayor made it to the top and the first glass stone complete with artwork was well and truly laid. The second was out in the country near nowhere in particular almost opposite the site of the notorious guinea pig farm on Sudbury Road Newchurch. The original purpose of the building was as a school serving several country villages in the area, now after raising nearly £80,000 the Victorian building had been enhanced with new toilets, double glazing, central heating and re-equipment of rooms including the main hall. Well done the management committee, you have saved the old Victorian building from falling further into decay but keeping the building in constant use is certainly a job for the future.

Brighter Borough Presentation Evening

Who can remember the 50's and 60's when the only thing to brighten one's life on the street was that large poster showing that famous Guiness advert with a short stocky man carrying a large steel beam on his head with a toucan perched on the end? It is all about quality of life and nothing brightens a town in the spring and summer more than neat bright flower arrangements. It perks you up when you struggle by to work in the car. I'm glad to say the volunteer organisations as well as the experts get better and better at it every year. I would say in the morning it changes the nation's mood more than Terry Wogan in

the old days. So the annual Brighter Borough presentation evening at Byrkley Gardens sponsored by the Garden Centre together with the Burton Mail, with assistance from ESBC, is a special event to recognise those people and volunteer organisations, not the experts, who make their gardens beautiful for us all to enjoy. A splendid meal is put on first to get us in the mood, then the prizes, then a question and answer session by an expert from TV or radio. (yet another failed attempt to find out why my parsnips look more like multi-limbed jellyfish than perfect conic sections, still there's always next year). Yes all this does make a difference to our lives.

Aldi Store in Burton

We were honoured indeed to be asked to cut the red ribbon on the occasion of the opening of the new Aldi Store on Horninglow Road opposite the police station. The occasion was not without its humour but first to say we were most impressed by both the quality of what was on offer and the considerable sales expertise shown by the management. Despite there being a number of well inscribed silver pairs of scissors available in the Mayor's parlour I had forgotten to bring any of them. I just stood pressed against the wall holding in one hand one end of the tape ready to receive around 100 punters all fairly aggressively out for day-one bargains, and with a pair of plastic scissors borrowed from the shelves nervously gripped in the other hand. At the appointed second all the tills went clunk releasing money for change, the checkout team were ready and in response to a signal I cut the ribbon. The press surged forward, the lady quickly returned the scissors back on the shelf and all of a sudden the place was in business, complete with amazing offers. No-one had much time for the Mayor in all the confusion, but he must admit he had rather enjoyed the experience.

Church in Burton, Service of Blessing, Youth for Christ, The Tsunami appeal, Meeting the archbishop – a most unstuffy experience

Every year in the Town Hall a group of Burton Churches known as church in Burton get to combine on certain activities for the benefit of Burton. Their main objective is to see transformation in our town. We sang with the worship band, listened to readings and presentations on education, the council, government and justice, emergency services, business and for the disadvantaged, thanks from the mayor and all donations were to local charities.

I'll link this with a very active organisation in Burton called Burton Youth for Christ. Don't necessarily be put off by its name, through its arts outreach team it has for 20 years been supporting schools, doing youth and community

work and Church Youth programmes. It goes under lots of names, all bringing youth together with special emphasis on those with poor aspirations who might be in danger getting onto the streets. There is Stance, Reach, Blast, The Mix, Wrap – all names for the young not necessarily for us oldies to understand. We attended their production called 'Believe' on the 2nd March which was well supported by volunteers from Anglesey School, Paulet High School, and Paget High School 21 in all; youth in music and dance. They say 'Many young people we work with don't believe in their own abilities to achieve so our role is to accept them, believe in them and encourage them to maximise their individual potential.' We were all shocked at the disaster which occurred in the New Year following the Asian tsunami. The People from East Staffs had as usual helped by making contributions both locally and via the national aid agencies.

The Lions have contacts throughout the world and can guarantee money will arrive and be used properly, so we combined our effort with them. They had established contact with Lions Clubs in Sri Lanka who are best placed to understand local needs and to identify suitable life-sustaining projects. Following your kind donations we thought it appropriate to hold a thank-you evening at the Town Hall with performances from the Tutbury Band and Good Company, well done everyone who took part.

Life is full of surprises, we certainly received one when we met Archbishop Nichols to send off one stage from Burton as part of a round England cycle event to raise money for the Catenian Association. My expectations anyway were in terms of a gentleman somewhat venerable in a red cassock with cap to match as we awaited with Father McGinley for the cycle team outside St Modwen's Roman Catholic Church. I was right in the last of these only as round the corner they came; all in leotards including the archbishop together with several nuns and lay people. A very happy well organised team equipped with radio, cycling as a group along the byeways of England. Good luck to them.

Chapter 8

SPECIAL NEEDS CHILDREN

Crown School Street party and Anglesey Primary School centre for Dyslexic children (learning difficulties)

The event at Crown School was to congratulate Rachel Freeman on her retirement after no less than 28 years of service. We were pleased to take the opportunity of going round the school, talking to the staff and seeing the facilities they have available for children with very special needs. The town remains proud of the work Crown School does in easing the lives of these very special children. You will see later in these reports that the school also remarkably has a special relationship along with the Sea cadets and the Borough Council with the Navy, specifically HMS Victorious.

We attended the official opening of the new centre at Anglesey primary school for young children who are experiencing specific learning difficulties. This unit is an initiative by the Staffordshire county council. We were pleased to see that the latest whiteboard software is being used a teaching aid for dyslexia and for other aspects of this very difficult subject.

'Able To' Games (Disability Sport)

We attended the 'Able To' games at the Meadowside Leisure Centre for young handicapped people, sponsored by ESBC Sports Development. There is no doubt that the event was much enjoyed by all those who took part. (around 80 young people). Not only had the participants looked forward to the event, they were meeting new friends and having the pleasure of seeing the mayor (admittedly in polished black shoes) make a rubbish attempt in the penalty shootout. Full marks to those who gave up their Saturday organising and running the event both ESBC staff and others. In the nature of things those who came were willing but sometimes volatile and not always the easiest to handle. Well done to all the organisers.

Follow Your Dreams

Once again Burton was privileged to receive a visit from the fundraising 'Follow Your Dreams' team by kind permission of the Cooper's Square Management. The team travel the country raising funds for special needs children by selling

toys and other items. Whilst entertaining young people in the Shopping Centre they seek to raise general public's awareness of the needs of youngsters with learning difficulties. During their stay they receive regular visits by arrangement from special needs children from the various schools around Burton who are then well entertained by their team. Having attended their sessions more than once I would confirm they are a hard working group creating no nuisance by spending only a few days at each location before moving on to another shopping centre to further their good works.

The 'Uttoxeter Project'

There is a huge problem associated with accommodation for those with mental and similar problems when the time comes for them to be brought back into the community. Finding a suitable site for housing with warden control for this is very difficult. The site at the end of Bradley Street in Uttoxeter is just within the shopping area but near to the doctors and police if they are needed. However no-one wants to live next door with a young family and in this case their neighbours are the bus station on one side and on the other the next shop down the High Street. It had been discussed for around five years as The Uttoxeter Project and in the end Walbrook Housing Association made definite proposals. The property needed much refurbishment and conversion into separate small units. This came under considerable discussion in planning but in the end it all went through, the work was done and we were asked to open the project. At least it served to improve what was a very tatty corner round from the bus station. Previously the end wall of the old building had been shored up for years making it one of the worst eyesores in town. All this completed I must say it was with some misgivings that I grabbed the old spade to plant the inaugural tree, what made it worse was that it was within sight of our house and if it failed it would be there as a more or less permanent monument to something that was not quite right. In the end it all would depend on the quality of the site staff. After the planting we took the opportunity to stress the importance of their wardens making a strong effort to get to know the local people before rather than after any incident occurred. Would you believe thanks to some very professional handling there has been no trouble whatsoever since. (although I do have one finger crossed under this table as I type).

Training for school leavers, JHP, Connexions

We were then pleased to attend three more functions in Burton, the main object of these initiatives being to help school leavers either to find training or a job; focussing on those vulnerable young people who might have limited aspirations at the time and as such are in danger of finding themselves out on the streets in the wrong company. This is bad for themselves and also for the community.

The first was the presentation evening held at JHP training. Their objective is to help school leavers find work by pushing them in a friendly way towards work placements and nationally recognized qualifications. Any initiative to keep young people off the roads is to be applauded.

The second was the launch of Connexions in the old Post Office on New Street. The event was lively to say the least, we were moved out onto the pavement, we soon realised why – you can't make that scale of noise inside without damaging something. For once there was nowhere for John the chauffeur to hide so whereas I got a kind of bongo drum to bang on and he got the curious looking pipe. We were very soon joined by the noisy professionals who soon had us jumping up and down in a huge deluge of sound. The contribution from the bongo drum and the pipe was negligible. Several buses passed by, heads were turned but fortunately none contained a Mail photographer. When at last the noise stopped, with insides still vibrating (the oldies just can't take it) I was able to go inside and meet some of the young people who were being made welcome and signed in by the new staff. Its position on New Street is good for acting as a kind of friendly refuge and to provide proper help during that critical time when certain young people are either not at school for some reason or are out looking for a job.

I believe we need to be realistic in these cases and avoid the superlatives; if these initiatives are only partially successful they will have succeeded in making certain young peoples' lives happier and hopefully keep a good proportion of them off the streets.

The third was a visit to the Substance Misuse, BAC and O'Conner Centre for rehabilitation of ex prison inmates

It was a privilege for us to visit the Centre and to talk to Noreen Langan about how they are assisting drug and alcohol offenders (substance misusers) recover to normal life after a spell in prison and to chat a little to some of the 'inmates.' Obviously they work closely with the Prison Service. This is a vital service which effects all of East Staffs country and town areas alike. Often such offenders relapse after release and families suffer as well. Apparently they often attribute this to lack of support. The Centre aims to provide this in a constructive manner.

I must say at this stage I had a strange feeling and the ghosts of the past came flooding back. 126 Station street and next door were in the old days, believe it or not, used as the famous Allied Breweries lunch clubs (Basses had the same down the road) and were the scene of much pleasurable feasting and drinking during lunch breaks. I could just still imagine the smell of the joints as they emerged from the oven for carving, the chatting over a glass or two and the return to work in good fettle. Of course this all came to an end when brewery fortunes declined rapidly in the 80's but the memory still lingered. Strangely enough when Coors took over, the houses were forgotten and left empty for some years rotting away. When discovered they were passed over for this very good cause to do their bit to solve one of today's serious social problems at least drugs which simply did not exist in Burton in the 70's.

Chapter 9

OPPORTUNITIES FOR YOUNG PEOPLE

From 'Surely Not Girls Rugby!' to the Rugby World Cup.

Seven-a-side soccer is very popular and has now become the major pastime for both schoolboys and schoolgirls all over the country. I recall the organising of half a dozen pitches and 20 odd teams recently formed the backbone of the new style Uttoxeter Carnival. Things are very much on-going. I do wish however that some supporter-parents would keep themselves a little more under control. If little Gary did to Little Joseph what Gary's dad suggested so loudly and without fear of contradiction from the touchline, I fear there would be no alternative but to put the game henceforth in the hands of the police; and all this is for the under tens!

This apart I was pleased to visit Burton Rugby Club one bitterly cold afternoon to be introduced to the Burton area inter-schools girls rugby tournament. After my quiet upbringing in the 1950's where girl's schools were invariably hidden behind a Colditz style five metre wall this kind of thing – even after 50 years or so – was clearly quite outside my sphere of experience up to then. I was straight away amazed and pleased to see how much all concerned were thoroughly enjoying themselves. Sometimes a 'tag' was more of a trip leaving some girl flat in the mud but then up and away for more! Later by the time the final was played across the other side of the field, when I was waiting to present the winners' prizes the chill was setting in from my toes upwards!. No-one was complaining however so I kept quiet and watched more of the frequent mud splattering and general pressing into the mire which is part of what was clearly described as a 'non-contact' sport. Burton Rugby Club were to be applauded for allowing the girls to play on their first team pitch particularly after the recent heavy rains.

This notwithstanding Burton Rugby Club went from strength to strength during the year, with the first XV gaining promotion to Midlands 2 West and the ladies XV to Midland 2 respectively. We were pleased to attend a civic reception on the eighth of September to celebrate their success.

The club's commitment to the Sure Sport project, a partnership between East Staffs Borough Council, Leander rowing club, Burton Albion football club and the rugby club to link these sports clubs with local schools and to provide opportunities for young people to experience top-class sport coaching has been admirable.

So England won the World Cup and brought the famous trophy back to the UK. Very creditably they refused to take the safe option and lock the trophy away but instead took it round the country for display at various rugby clubs. So on a cold but sunny morning we awaited the arrival of two identical land Rovers one of which held the famous trophy. They proceeded along the agreed route at the front of the stand, turned round and there it was; the trophy plus a special stand to put it on for photos. In the meantime over 100 young rugby players awaited in turn for their chance to be photographed with the trophy. What a brilliant opportunity for such a photograph pinned to any club wall. Although the trophy remained at Burton for only one hour, thanks to excellent organisation all the business was satisfactorily completed within that time. Well done Burton Rugby club.

International Scout and Guide fellowship St George's parade

We were pleased to entertain two Swedish members of the International Scout and Guide fellowship at the town hall. Yvonne and Gjermund Austvick (Yvonne in spectacular traditional costume) who are members of St George's Guild in Sweden which is twinned with the Trefoil Guild in Burton, were here attending an international Scout and guide fellowship conference in Kent. The couple spent a few days with members of Burton's trefoil Guild (an organisation of former guides) and were later taken to the National Memorial Arboretum in Alrewas together with Coors visitor centre.

This was followed on the 17th April by the St George's parade. A magnificent turnout of young people packing the United Methodist and United Reform Church on George Street almost up to the rafters with beavers, cub scouts, scouts and guides! Thanks to Rev Peter Howard for having us and the Rev Colin Meynall for his inspiring address, all well worth me turning out in full mayoral dress for such a memorable occasion!

Chicage Rock Café

A visit to Luminaz at the Chicago Rock Café can be counted as the most 'down and out, feeling completely out of touch' event I attended during my year in office but in the end I was saved by a nice man and all was safe and sound. The chauffeur John, wisely as at turned out, refused to accompany me as I approached the café to the first blast of music on time at 8 pm.

A pint of lager was thrust at me and I was advised that there was to be a live rock band competition and apparently I was to be a judge.

The music from the stage then went on for hours louder and louder without any known progress on the competition. They were just warming up. I wondered why I was there. Perhaps it was to attract more customers in but I didn't think so. I was rather overdressed, anyway I was sitting discretely to one side out of the way of the customers, really I suppose so as not to attract attention, being asked to dance or something.

Clearly I had no idea whatsoever of any difference between the contestants, after a while my senses were too numb to appreciate anything. Eventually a really nice man from Radio Derby (they are all nice from Radio Derby I know from experience) rescued me by sitting down beside me and saying he was also a judge.(phew) When it came time to make a final decision at about midnight from around eight bands contesting, the mike was passed over for comments on each. I quickly passed it over to my friend. I think he grabbed it actually, we had got friendly but he did see my predicament. Brilliantly he then proceeded to talk coolly, intelligently and politely on each band, encouraging them in a friendly manner and picking out the best. I left out into the night both mind-blown and staggered at his eloquence to the car where John had been quietly enjoying the evening.

British Championships rhythmic gymnastics, Youth Games for Special Schools, Partnership Youth Games, Lichfield Cathedral Youth Events, Duke of Edinburgh's Award Scheme, Army cadets at Knook camp

On a quite different (quieter) scale of things it is surprising what events come to Burton. On the 26th of November Meadowside hosted the British Championships for **Rhythmic Gymnastics**. The sport was quite unknown to me, girls from all parts of the country took part (in 4 categories under 10, under 12, junior and senior) doing clever tricks combined with gymnastics using various items of equipment which I would describe as hoops, small sized beach balls and short sticks with ribbons attached. (the official titles were rope, ball, clubs, ribbons and hoop). The sort of thing that clever young girls, after hours and hours practice, can achieve sometimes in the privacy of their home or gym but would find quite impossible on their own with 200 critical people watching. Their efforts and success rate was very impressive. Well done Meadowside for obtaining this event.

ESBC in conjunction with Sport across Staffordshire and Sport England hosted both **Youth Games for Special Schools** on the 9th June and **Partnership Youth Games** on the 12th of June. Whereas it may be somewhat horrifying for a new mayor to be required to speak a few words to 1500 young people, one can only be proud of the efforts of our professional team at Shobnall Leisure Centre in organising both these events with such efficiency.

Of particular merit was the attendance of various successful present athletes who talked to the young people acting as role models for the day. We returned proud of the way ESBC had conducted these events.

A further notable sporting event took place later in the year when at the town Hall we attended the presentation of the **Sports Scholarship awards 2004**. No less than 71 athletes and five coaches received scholarships awards. Many of our elite athletes were presently either representing their country or in national development squads, underlining the surprising sporting quality we have within East Staffs.

We very much enjoyed attending functions in **Lichfield Cathedral** put on by various youth groups supported by the cathedral.

We were pleased to attend the event 'Rice is Life' including one item from Burton performed by 'One Nation' Plus 'Boystruz Blast' from Arts Project Wrap, the event being sponsored by the Staffordshire Youth Service in Lichfield Cathedral in conjunction with Staffordshire performing arts also 'Music Share' at which Rolleston and Burton schools took part.

We saw how the cathedral, thanks to clever introduction of props including a performing stage and turning round the seating, was transformed into a beautiful venue for young people to perform their various skills.

The **Duke of Edinbugh's award scheme** is organised in East Staffordshire by a common committee in Burton (De Ferrer's Open Award Committee) and a separate committee in Uttoxeter (based at Thomas Alleyne's School). We were pleased to visit both organisations at various times to view progress and to present bronze, silver and gold awards.

These awards are tough but fair and there is no doubt that the comparatively few young people who attend (compared with full school numbers) get much out of their experiences. As always it depends upon the organisers who give up their time to take on this responsibility which inevitably increases year by year with the rise of the 'suing culture.'

I learnt how tough when we went to Longnor to see off a group of young people from De Ferrer's Open Award Centre doing their assessment walk. They were ready to go and I casually thought to help a young girl (weighing I should say around 9 stone) to pick up her bergen. (that's what they call a rucksack in the army) As I nearly fell over with the weight I enquired if it did not hurt carrying such loads even with some soft rubber under the shoulder straps. I was advised – not after the first half hour!

The organisers then had a clever way of checking their progress whilst at the same time in a nearby hostelry partaking of some of the famous local chocolate cake. I must say, not being in walking kit, we also found the cake delicious. Long may this continue.

The visit to the army cadets annual camp at **Knook**, near Salisbury Plain was a real eye-opener for us. We went to support cadets from Uttoxeter at their annual camp. These cadets up to the age of 17 are a strong source of recruits for the army. Any of them could be sent to Iraq within six months should they reach the required age for joining the army. Groups were almost 30/80 girls and boys, all were subjected to the same fairly tough training exercises. (for me they would be very tough if not impossible).

Of course there is a fair amount of danger associated with this kind of training otherwise there would be no point in doing it. The responsibility for this lies with the supervisors who give up their spare time (which is paid) for this purpose. According present day practice they do fill out risk analysis forms and clear paperwork properly which seems quite onerous. They ride in tanks, fire weapons, go round battle training courses and sometimes make special visits such as going to the battlefields in France. Again the ultimate success and state of readiness of the British army will depend on the volunteer soldiers such as these who are prepared to join and do this training, good luck to them.

Carers Association for southern Staffordshire (CASS)

Sometimes a surprise awaits. This certainly was the case when we attended a **CASS** carers 'chill out' event week at the Brewhouse arts Centre. Their objectives are to help carers who can be any member of our society. We think of grown-ups helping old people but there are also young boys and girls at school caring for parents and old people caring for young people. The possibilities have no end but nevertheless CASS have an objective to help carers by giving them a chance to relax and chill out, to have a break and talk problems out between themselves and to take advantage of a range of complementary therapies and pampering treatments. Following discussions with Jill Wyatt and Cynthia Bowden we were pleased to accept their organisation as one of the mayor's charities and also to invite them to our civic insignia on 22nd September. Later on the 30th December CASS arranged the Christmas party for around 125 young carers at the Universal Function Suite in Stafford. I was amazed by the organisation required to transport this number of young people each from a different address both to and from the event. This event was special and as CASS was one of our official charities we were able to take some money early from the funds available in order that the Mayoress could augment the presents for the children. I believe the event was a huge success.

Jigsaw, Young people's holiday events Meadowside, Canterbury Road and Rocester

On the 30th October we attended the **Jigsaw** mentoring partnership graduation ceremony. This is perhaps the most famous of the volunteer operations in the town. Many quite notable members of Burton society have in the past taken on mentoring responsibilities, helping young people including members of the ethnic community. Help is given by means of friendly discussions at regular intervals at venues convenient to all parties. One of the objectives is that in the end mentees are able to obtain equal access for opportunities and do not suffer through ignorance of their rights to become self-reliant members of society. On this occasion six mentees were officially graduating, please keep going Jigsaw.

ESBC provide a programme of events during the holidays to reduce stress on young mothers and fathers by providing constructive entertainment for their children. We attended this event, held on the wash lands behind **Meadowside** leisure centre. There was a good turnout of parents and children, all enjoying themselves as they have done for the past 10 years since this event was first provided. I noticed according to the literature that allowance is made for what is described as a 'free play opportunity' for the under 11's and their families – what a relief for them! A similar event was held on the newly refurbished community Park off **Canterbury Road** and Melbourne Avenue on the 24th of July. We were also pleased to open the new skate board and kiddies play park also facilities at **Rocester** Recreation ground on the 8th September.

Noise Action Day and *Green and Keen* awards

Now the problem of **noise**. I was pleased to present prizes to winning pupils and runners up for the 'design a poster' competition. These posters will be displayed around the town and follow receipt of over 500 noise complaints every year. These vary from noisy animals in many cases due to poor attention, loud music which is played by the young without regard to reduced tolerance levels shown by older folk, intruder alarms and even DIY works. I could not help thinking that some reluctant DIY workers might be glad to down tools following such a complaint. Some councillors themselves might even be said to make too much noise which I suppose they would describe as part of the job.

However noise remains a serious business and a daily nuisance to many people. Nowadays peoples' volume of activity is increased and so is the number of vehicles on the road.

For the second year voluntary groups and schools were recognized with **Green and Keen** awards for their environmental projects with Burton Conservation Volunteers (for their sterling work on the overgrown banks at Branston Waterpark) together with Violet Lane infants School and St Peters first school all receiving awards.

Amateur Dramatics in Burton

One of the quiet successes in Burton is the number of amateur drama groups performing both in the Brewhouse Theatre and in the case of the Operatic Society at DeFerrers Specialist Technology College. Some of this talent is thanks to the Anne Lee School of Music and Dance which has been going now for nearly 20 years. This is especially notable as you may guess historically Burton had not been noted for the arts; some would say more for pushing beer barrels about. In addition her efforts and those of her team put in over the past 20 years or so have done much to improve the self esteem of local young people along with their career expectations in all sorts of directions whatever it they may be. We were pleased to attend their production of 'Oliver at Yuletide' on the 16th of December followed by the unbelievable six pantomimes in one day for the Tsunami appeal on 22nd January. A number of these young people pass onto local theatre groups and even occasionally into the wider field of entertainment, long may she continue.

Whenever we were able we were pleased to attend productions by amateur groups at the Brewhouse and elsewhere. Audience numbers at the Brewhouse are very appropriate for productions of this kind in terms of making a profit and also give local groups the opportunity of performing to a fairly high standard.

The productions of 'Shirley Valentine, 'Blood Brothers' and 'Oliver' by the Little Theatre company were enjoyed by all those who attended as were 'Half a Sixpence' and 'Dolly's to Follies' by Mellow dramatics and on a slightly different theme 'Music and Love' sponsored by Soroptimist International of Burton on Trent and especially 'Annie' and 'The Wizard of Oz' by the Operatic Society at de Ferrers and 'A Few of our favourite Things' by Branston Drama Group later in the year.

Whenever possible, and with permission, we liked to go backstage after performances to chat to the cast, hopefully fully dressed (this was checked beforehand) to thank them for their special efforts.

I was privileged during my time in office to be a member of the BDAC (the Burton and district arts Council) whose job it is to allocate the available grant finance for the arts by means of bursaries to individuals, the Brewhouse and elsewhere as well as to oversee the annual Competitive Vocal Festival held on 6th March together with splendid events such as 'celebrating music 2004' sponsored by the Burton Mail. This consisted of week-long contributions to music from no less than 20 Burton schools and The Burton Music Centre's Annual Concert on the 21st March which included a brilliant performance from Burton Youth Jazz Orchestra. Their aim is to show the musical talent available in schools from both Burton and Uttoxeter.

We then attended Abbot Beynes School Arts College on 1st March to look round a small sculptures Exhibition by James Butler RA. He is famous in town for sculpting 'The Cooper' now in Cooper's square. A miniature of which was presented to our very long standing Chief Executive William Saunders on his recent retirement.

BDAC were a small group which did much to quietly facilitate arts in Burton particularly by putting finance in the areas where it was most needed.

Chapter 10

Soccer events around the Borough

Bass Charity Vase

The Bass Charity Vase football competition is special and unique to Burton. It dates back further than the FA Cup and is played between the Albion and local teams mostly from the football league. Traditionally it is held as a tournament prior to the start of the British football season. The trophy consists of a splendid silver vase on a large tapering plinth which is needed to show all the shields depicting the winners over the years. It is kept in a large wooden box, opened with quiet ceremony once a year for presentation after the final tie.

One of the objects of these matches originally was to ensure players were fit for the coming season; nowadays we presume all these expensive players are tied to rigorous training schedules but they are young, sexy and human so what do you expect?

Such is the special reputation of this our football competition that as recently as 2004 clubs such as Derby County, Stoke City, Notts County, Nottingham Forest, West Bromwich Albion, Gresley Rovers, and Rocester were prepared to send representative teams.

The main object of course is to collect money for charity and Messrs Mellor, Peck and Fairbrother together with their dedicated assistants have had much success in this over the years, previously in 2003 they were able to donate goods to the value of no less than £10,000 to local charities and worthwhile causes.

They also have the responsibility to ensure that the necessary organisation is properly carried out and that the local grounds at Gresley Rovers and Rocester as well as the Pirelli Stadium are available.

Not to say that these football league sides don't have substitutes, I noticed when Nottingham Forest reached the final their players' average size increased by three inches in height and around half a stone of solid muscle in the second half to ensure victory.

May I thank the Bass Charity Vase committee for receiving us so kindly at all the matches after which we had the opportunity of meeting players and officials and local supporters. I must say that referees and assistant referees do a fine job on the pitch but I did notice that socially some of them 'take no prisoners.'

It is remarkable that this competition has survived thus far into the days of big money football. Each year it gets more and more difficult to attract the big teams to Burton but thanks to the efforts of the organising committee who look after the sides so well, this tournament which is one of the oldest in football continues to thrive, long may it be so.

Strange Happenings at the Rams

Normally this would not be included as it was an invitation from Derby City Council to see the Rams play bottom of the table Rotherham United. The glossy programme was full of the recent memorial service to Brian Clough at the stadium with Nigel Clough present, so perhaps this is enough excuse to tell the story.

We were kindly placed behind glass in the west stand Toyota executive box and well entertained in comfortable surroundings with the Lord Mayor of Derby in full attendance. She was a middle-aged lady, I would say with presumption possibly not possessing the greatest sense of humour. I guessed she might have played centre forward very well for Derby in the surroundings of the City Council Chamber but not I suspect necessarily on the football field.

When the game started we all ventured outside out onto the terrace, which nowadays as you probably know means sitting fairly close together on plastic seats side by side. I sat down out of politeness next to the good lady who seemed to be sitting on her own, just as Rotherham slotted in their first goal, greeted by a stony silence from the Derby supporters. This was shortly followed by the second which I admit tended to kill conversation, we could hear an angry murmur of frustration going round the ground. When the third went in I felt positively sorry for the lady and rapidly went through all the good things about Derby I could think of, to try to cheer her up, but as she had not started too cheerful anyway this was proving difficult. Time went on and good things to say about Derby had almost dried up, the situation began to feel hopeless. I was desperately thinking what to say next when Derby unexpectedly scored, the crowd erupted loudly and without thinking I gave her a real hug.

In first retrospect I was somewhat embarrassed by this, we all do things on impulse at times but suppose Derby scored again? Of course they did, so I was forced to hand out another, phew – surely that would be the end of the matter, but no almost in the last minute Derby slotted in the winer and the crowd were in absolute uproar when I dished out my third and last hug of the afternoon.

Chapter 11

MILITARY MATTERS

Royal British Legion group annual church and Remembrance Day parades and poppy appeal, Army benevolent fund, Friends of the Staffordshire Regiment, 60th Anniversary of D Day Landings,

We were proud to attend these events organised by the Royal British Legion, the army, fire and rescue and the navy.

The objectives of the Legion are to help those who fought in wars, to care for widows and other dependants and for the growth of comradeship amongst all its members. Time moves on however and numbers become reduced for this reason alone. I should like to pay tribute to Ken and Anne Compton together with their team both for their kindness to us and for the wonderful work they have done to keep the groups in Burton and Uttoxeter together. This year's Poppy appeal which we were honoured to launch raised in excess of £21,000 an increase of 20% on the previous year. Without their efforts I believe the veterans would be too few in number to continue to put on a proud annual church parade such as this.

I believe sympathy for the men and women of the Royal British Legion and for their objectives is now increasing, it was particularly good to see the turnout of students from Burton College outside the War Memorial on Remembrance Day and full marks to the young boy from school who played the last Post so competently. I believe the new dividing wall with a chain is to be erected around the war memorial to better define the area.

The organisation which supports many serving and former soldiers and their families is the Army benevolent fund. We were pleased to join them on Sunday 5th of December for their famous annual curry lunch at the Army training Regiment Whittington barracks. Talking to them we learn that the days of the old county regiments are numbered. Of course old links will be preserved but the new British Army will certainly be based on function rather than a throwback from the old recruiting areas. We must never forget however the great contribution that regiments like the Stafford's made in the two world wars.

On 21st March we attended the AGM of the Burton Branch of the Friends of the Staffordshire Regiment.

This meeting I shall never forget in that following the normal agenda we were shown a series of rocket powered grenades of various types which had killed and were killing so many soldiers and others in Northern Island, the Middle East, Afghanistan and elsewhere. These were fearsome weapons lightweight, capable of penetrating vehicles and being fired hand-held. A sobering thought, thanks for the demo.

23rd October was special. It was the 60th anniversary of D Day and practically it was the last time that due to age comrades who took part could be present in Normandy to celebrate. It was held at Coors visitor centre for the general public. Amongst various interesting exhibits of a military nature were some young soldiers including one in desert kit. I spoke to him and he said he was a local man recently returned from Iraq. I was proud of what he had achieved but somewhat surprised at his young age. Apparently when the regiment goes overseas they all go irrespective of age or length of service, I expect they know what they are doing.

'Happy birthday Glen' Concert

On a happier note we attended the 'Happy Birthday Glen' (Miller) concert at Repton School. The concert was enjoyable notable as the one time the mayor arrived late due to misunderstanding on start time. However not to worry recent heavy rains had caused much flooding along the causeway and when we arrived this was assumed to be the reason, the concert having started there was really no time to offer any further explanation. Thank you Rotary Club of Burton, proceeds were to Burton Cancer Ward Appeal.

Suez 1952

Whatever has the Suez campaign got to do with all this? Sometimes strange things do happen.

At the beginning of my year as Mayor of the Borough I had attended an event in the council chamber at Stoke when the Lord Mayor had distributed medals to a group of ex-servicemen who were in the Canal zone prior to its occupation in 1952 and who for some reason had not received medals now over 50 years had passed.

Apparently (and this is where we retreat into the realms of fantasy) because no one had asked the War Office for medals then consequently no response had been received. Had a request been made at that time it would very likely have been refused and this would have been strictly the end of the matter. As it was with politics changing over the past 50 years the powers that be had softened, the request had been made, and it was decided that medals after all would be issued.

At Stoke I must admit there was complete confusion but at no fault of the Lord Mayor. The receipt of the medals had not been co-ordinated. Some were given with clasps some without clasps, some with ribbons some without, there was even a question who had to pay for the ribbons if they were more than a certain length! I had really had had enough of this shambles so at the end of the proceedings I approached the man in charge and politely offered to officially present any outstanding medals to old soldiers from East Staffordshire back in our Council Chamber.

To my surprise later I received a message that there were in fact six old soldiers due for their medals so we accordingly set up for an official presentation.

I felt rather humble presenting these complimenting them especially on their patience over the past 50 years. Then perhaps rashly thought it was the least I could do to ask if there was anything I could do for them. At which I was told no thank you then was further humbled by the gift of a nice bottle of whisky (which in those days I enjoyed). Typical I thought of the National Serviceman of the 1950s.

Staffs Fire and Rescue Service

As regards our Fire and Rescue Service we were privileged to attend two passing out ceremonies, both were in line with recent policies.

The first passing out parade involved 10 young people, nine boys and one girl who were taken on by the fire service for a course lasting 12 weeks. These young people were failing at school for various reasons and had been let off school one day per week to attend the course. This was carried out on strictly military lines and covered such items as fire pumps, visit to ambulance HQ, community based fire safety, road safety, breathing apparatus and so on. Classes were taken by firefighters on their days off who naturally found the young people in difficult to handle especially at the start of the course. Military discipline (which this kind of youngster often appreciates) helped but at the end of the course many of the instructing team told me, with a sigh that told it all, that they would never do it again. I then spent some little time advising them that what they had done was very much worthwhile for the community and please would they change their minds. I do hope I was at least partially successful in this. In the end the young people gave quite a good account of themselves on the presentation day. They had seen the benefits of the course whilst in the meantime it was the firefighters instructing who had done the hard work and no doubt suffered some abuse.

The second passing out parade, which those present are unlikely to forget, was following the end of the standard 12 week training course for individuals wanting to join the service as firefighters, after which they are designated to join teams at various stations around the county. As usual invitations were issued to parents and local officials to attend the presentation day, which I accordingly attended. Turnout was good and the firefighter's squad performed very adequately on the pumping exercise including firing water on a simulated four-storey building.

The final demonstration was extracting simulated casualties from vehicles following a road accident. For this purpose a rather battered Austin Metro and what appeared to be a brand new light green Jaguar was brought on to the parade ground. The Jaguar had already caused some comment. The assumption amongst the assembled company was that it was in some way defective or incomplete, many of us thought it had no engine. However assumptions proved incorrect as we could see it was being driven in the normal manner. For the purposes of the trial dummies were then placed under the Metro and inside the Jaguar. Air bags were then placed under the Metro which enabled dummies under the car to be removed. The best was left until last.

First one of the firefighters approached the Jaguar with a heavy wrench and smashed each window in turn. The onlookers including myself were amazed that such damage was necessary to the car – several were offering their car in exchange when the hydraulic metal cutter appeared, and in no time cut through the 4 roof supports, leaving the car's roof a mass of twisted metal on the floor. As the dummy was removed you could hear a sort of strangled gasp going through the audience. This included several of the senior supervisors who were not informed of the arrangement with the manufacturers. Apparently this car, following some severe runs on their test track, was not suitable for road use and could be destroyed 'provided all the pieces were returned!' In response to a politely worded question the reply was 'we need to know how to attend to vehicles with the latest high tech alarms and security systems.'

This remained a talking point for months – if you met a young fireman just out of training you could ask him were you there on that day when …?

Families, affiliations and *HMS Victorious*

In 1970 I had worked in Barrow in Furness during the time of the launch of *HMS Resolution*, the UK's first Polaris submarine. After an ignominious start when the boat (all submarines are boats) ended up on a sandbank on launch due to the changing tide following some delaying tactics by nuclear protesters (this kind of thing could be hushed up in those days) *HMS Resolution* and at her sister submarines had done their bit in keeping the peace for the next 34 years; however controversial this might have been. In those days I could never imagine I should ever be allowed near, let alone inside, such a vessel.

This link with the navy and recently with submarines was started originally by Burton Sea cadets whom I am pleased to say participate in these visits and go aboard the submarines. I had been over to inspect them at their barracks on Stapenhill Road on 5th February and had noted their first class turnout.

Now we had come full circle. We had received this splendid invitation for families and others to visit *HMS Victorious* being one of our four present Trident submarines. This would be just prior to its full overhaul which would take over one year including replacement of nuclear fuel which was amazingly scheduled to last for the rest of its service life.

We arrived at Helensburgh Pier at the allotted time together with crew family members, several disabled children and that nice lady from Crown School, whose name I'm afraid I cannot remember; Crown School always entertain the navy during their reciprocal visits to Burton. We were surprised to find the boat not there. Not to worry a fleet tender shortly arrived to take us out to the submarine moored in the middle of the loch with police boats buzzing around as security; this looked decidedly serious.

We climbed down inside through a manhole in the top of the hull and were amazed at the size of the vessel, being as tall as a three-storey house. We were greeted warmly in the spacious wardroom. I had time only to note the depth gauge reading around three metres, eventually appreciating we were under the sea even whilst on the surface, when the captain announced we would be sailing in 10 minutes! This was not what I was expecting, however we set out on a short cruise lasting around half an hour during which we were kindly shown round the vessel, ending up in the control room. Yes the days of peering through the periscope with cap turned back to front were well and truly over, now they sat back and looked at multiple TV screens. We now proceeded on the surface through the loch and were again most privileged to climb several vertical ladders up to the top of the fin. Here the Mayoress did exceptionally well and we ended up crushed together looking through a small manhole at the top supervised by a young seaman standing above us making sure we got up to no monkey business. The view across the loch was magnificent. We later supported them by witnessing their decommissioning ceremony before *HMS Victorious* left for overhaul, dinner guests including a magnificent 'who's who' in the navy, truly memorable occasions.

Chapter 12

THE ETHNIC COMMUNITY

Community Centre, Pakistani, Afgan Groups, Chinese New Year

The Festival of Learning was the first many visits we made to meet the ethnic group at the **Community Centre** in Uxbridge Street. As always we received a warm welcome, this event celebrated 'adult learners week.' We were shown the various facilities including computers, which have been made available for adult learning in the centre. The event was organised by Mohammed Jamil who fronts events for this group. Also noted is the help given by representatives from the County Council and the Police Liaison Officer during events such as this to ensure their success.

Amongst other the events attended were on the 14th August the launch of 'Central Youth,' one of the aims being to raise funds for the victims of the recent Bangladesh Flood Disaster, an Eid party on 20th November for presentation of cheque and raising further funds for the same purpose and on the 22nd December a presentation on 'Community Learning and learning from each other.' The Centre is next to their mosque on Uxbridge Street and both are fully integrated in their activities. Like most communities they have their difficulties, however we found them to be friendly, peaceful and a positive part of our community well supported by the help offered.

The **Afghan** Society are comparatively new to Burton. In the past their men have come over alone, now their wives are beginning to accompany them. In many cases they came fleeing from the Taliban which still remain an extremist Moslem group in Afghanistan. Indeed they used to rule their country. I believe extremist groups to be poison in any community as they do not tolerate others either of a different belief or those of the same belief who do not practise in the way they do.

Anyway we are pleased to accept these new residents as part of our

~ WARM RECEPTION! ~

community and to this end we attended their celebration at the Caribbean Association just down the road on 6th February. Thanks to Geoff Noble from Staffs CC. who helped promote this event. The Centre was packed as other nationals were bussed in from elsewhere. We heard speeches and listened to music, they were polite and easy to talk to within the constraints of language. Local employers, particularly Kerry Foods value their work and increasingly are moving them into managerial positions.

In the old days in the desert for a while I was privileged to have a formidable Afgan driver called Ataula Jan. He wore the traditional floppy hat, baggy trousers and decorated shoes of his race. During one leave he asked me to buy him a pair of binoculars, after a while I asked him politely 'what do you want those for in the desert?' He said 'to see Russians;' notably within a few years the Afgans had sent them packing out of their country with a bloody nose.

By now the Wing Wah on New Street has already become an institution in the town with its special choice of dishes, although competition is always available. We were delighted to attend their **Chinese new year celebrations** on 7th February and were surprised to see so many of our Chinese friends from Uttoxeter sharing the event with us, complete with dragon with long tail and large mouth preceded with man with small fly on stick.

New Horizons Celebration Event, One World Week in Burton, Visit to Sikh Community Celebration, and Launch of interfaith Network

Then there was a very special first-time event mainly for local women from India held at Anglesey School in partnership with Wedgewood Memorial College and which formed part of **New Horizon's** policy of bringing skills to the community. This event followed a residential learning programme for Asian women and their children at the Wedgewood Memorial College at Barleston at which a number of local Indian ladies attended. This may seem of very small importance to us but many Asian women living locally are kept too much in the home compared with normal western standards and are unable to take advantage of local facilities and as such to better integrate into the community.

Of course we must all come together and 'share our similarities,' this was brought out in our **One World Week** Interfaith Meeting in the Town Hall on January 19th instigated once again by Syd Bill who does so much to bring different faiths together in this town. We heard from those who have experience of interfaith in other communities and from the hospital where local developments serve all faiths. More suggestions were needed on how the Network can move forward.

I was pleased again with the kind assistance of Syd Bill to visit the **Sikh** community on 15th October. We received a very friendly reception during which I met Walia H Singh, Manjit Sinjh and other prominent members of the Sikh Community. This was followed by a satisfying meal then into worship with heads covered and shoes off. First a monetary offering to the priest then with women on the left, men on the right to sit on the floor whilst the priest read from their holy book accompanied by music. I found this most soothing and, together with friendly chatter afterwards, a very favourable experience.

Clearly they do form an important part of our community here in Burton. I will admit however to some practice at floor-sitting just before the event did pay dividends.

Also to mention the Part that Syd Bill has taken in the launch of the **interfaith network**. Its meeting at the Town Hall on the 9th October included members of the Muslim, Christian, Quaker, humanist and Hindu faiths.

Chilly time for the Mayoress down Uxbridge Street

Of course nothing can be done about the weather except to say it can be unpredictable. One event which required considerable stamina, well beyond the call of duty on the part of the Mayoress, was following an invitation received a during the Christmas holiday to support an ethnic event (mostly for the Indian and Pakistani women) at the community centre down Uxbridge Street.

We always looked forward to these events as we were always politely received and our visits were much appreciated. It was basically about fund raising in Bangladesh. Anyway on this occasion the mayoress had obtained a sari for the event which came together with instructions from daughter-in-law (who originated in that part of the world) on how to wear it.

We had been at a previous event that morning opening the Christmas festivities in the Market Place which had been none too warm and had returned to the Town Hall to change. Being the holiday period there was no heating on in the Town Hall and it was bitterly cold. The mayoress was brave enough to put on her sari and was already much feeling the cold when we set off for Uxbridge Street. However her outfit was very well received by the local ladies and we were pleased to sit on chairs in the centre of the room not too far from the heaters. Then came the final straw when our chairs were changed to some next to the window that had been brought in freshly chilled from being stored outside in the cold. I was feeling the chill through my thick suit, one can only imagine what it felt like in a sari with little or nothing round the middle! However in the end all was well and with the very best of intentions no-one can predict the weather and in any case the room soon warmed up thanks to what is known as 'body heat!'

Chapter 13

Queen's hospital & hospices

Queen's Hospital Cancer Ward

We were privileged to attend the official opening of the new cancer unit. This followed an amazing effort headed on by Mr Terry Tricker which achieved its target of no less than £1 million for much-needed improvements to our hospital which we note is now the largest employer in town.

Not forgetting of course the contribution made by Tony Mulcahy in his 'final' fundraising event – Love is all The Final Embrace – a tribute to the Master of Romance, Engelbert Humperdinck which was held at the Town Hall on Saturday 3rd July. There was not a dry eye in the house. Not forgetting also the Rotary club of Burton on Trent who kindly agreed to include this cause as one of the mayor's charities.

Education Centre

We attended the relaunch of the **Burton Education Centre** at the School of health Burton Hospital. This will form a valuable centre of learning within the hospital site and includes a first-class lecture theatre and other facilities.

There was also the Burton Hospitals NHS Trust Excellence Awards Ceremony on 25th February. This was notable in that, following the choice of winners chosen from all aspects of the work of the hospital, somebody then came in with a video camera to provide in each case a most sincere and entertaining profile. You could see from the reaction of the audience that those chosen were special people in the life of the hospital.

The Country's First First Responder

Neill Phillips was not only Uttoxeter's **First Responder** he was the country's First Responder. Following his retirement he was provided with a civic reception in Uttoxeter Town Hall on 26th February. 'To commemorate Neill's retirement and publicly recognise his exceptional dedication to the people of our community.' He did the job on his own and did it well. His work continues but as is the way these days four good people have stepped into one man's shoes. Good luck to you Neill.

St Giles Hospice, St Katherine's Hospice, Hoar Cross Nursing Home and counting the coins for Donna Louise

We were pleased to support **St Giles** at their Sunflower Ball event, later to visit the hospice which is between Lichfield and Tamworth and on the 12th December to attend their most moving 'light up a life' service at Coors Visitor Centre. We are reminded that St Giles' catchment area includes all of East Staffordshire. A huge effort is required to raise the necessary finance which is done by no less than 750 volunteers and 11 charity shops across the region.

Katherine House Hospice which is the other similar facility serving East Staffs is situated by Stafford Hospital on Western Road Stafford. We were very grateful when they positively responded to our request to visit. Their problems are very similar, their standards are also very high but at times they remain disappointed that they cannot, through what appears to be an unnecessary red tape, take full advantage of the hospital facilities on to the adjoining site. Their catchment area is confined to Stafford and Uttoxeter and Burton and presumably the villages in between.

We also went to a fireworks party at Hoar Cross Nursing Home appropriately on 5th November. This seemed a happy place with many young relatives helping on the night, its location is however somewhat remote, these were the days before sat. navs. in the mayoral car. The fireworks could have been a useful aid to location but we arrived rather too early for this.

We were also invited to officially weigh the collection bucket for the **Donna Louise Trust** 'lose a pound for Christmas' appeal in Burton place shopping centre. We took advantage of an administrative error (arriving at first one week early) to have friendly cheer up chats with shoppers (with the chauffeur in fairly close attention) taking care to choose only the kind of pensioners who I thought might best do with a Christmas cheer up. As always local people were most friendly. We went again and contributions to the trust came to a splendid £130.52.

We also put a team for the Millionaires' Challenge at JCB organised by David Edwards. A very nice 'ordinary' but extraordinary person who is a local winner £1 million on Chris Tarrant's programme 'Who Wants to be a Millionaire.' For the sake of the trust, which he actively supports, he brought with him no less than three other super brains and raised £1500 on the night.

Whoever you are and whatever your family you never know when you may need their help.

CASES, Volunteers of Burton Hospitals, Alzheimers or Dementia and Diabetes

In future the volunteer bureau is to be known as **CASES**. Its function is to match individuals and groups who are interested in volunteering with suitable opportunities in the local communities. They will continue to stimulate and encourage local interest in volunteering and to develop opportunities for volunteering.

A good example of this was when previously, on 1st June, we had attended Queen's hospital to talk to the 'Volunteers of Burton hospitals.' They are most active in obtaining finance for specific hospital items and make themselves available at the entrance to the hospital most times during the day.

One thing we can easily forget about is the responsibility for the treatment of dementia, these days often called Alzheimer's. We attended a 'Yuletide Warmup' where Trish Slater the local Treasurer and co-organiser of the **Alzheimer's** Society Burton Carers Group had invited a number of people living locally who are affected by the disease in one way or another.

It is estimated that there are around 1600 people affected by the disease in the Staffordshire. Many are looked after by their partner whose responsibility of care may last years. They often need help, sometimes only a friendly voice is needed at to keep them going.

Then there was the Burton and District Children and Families group of **Diabetes UK** with their 'Party in the Park' at Belvedere Park. Their object was to raise money to put a smile back on the little ones' faces, also to hold education evenings. Good luck to them also.

The joy of Christmas, the hospital visit and the most unlucky man over Christmas 2004

One of the pleasures of the year was Christmas and all the efforts made by local organisations to help young people enjoy themselves as much as possible. The Burton Lions are well in the forefront of this and their famous Christmas tree in the shopping precinct invites many shoppers to obtain presents for charity. This is a monumental feat of organisation and I must say upstairs the site of an empty shop completely full of Christmas presents for local youngsters brought a tear to the eye. We had an official visit to the tree during which we were met by two well made up lions. It was a new experience getting into conversation with them – one being not quite as fierce with a young girl's voice coming out somewhere around the mane!

An extra joy during our visits to the shopping centres was the opportunity to talk to the old folks, parents and children, seeing in general what a friendly down-to-earth population including visitors there were in Burton over Christmas.

We thought we should do something at Queen's hospital to celebrate Christmas. However the last thing the hospital wants is official mayoral visits when they are short staffed and many patients have been sent home for the holiday period. So what to do? We contacted Terry Tricker who asked us if we wished to judge the Christmas trees. We said yes and he said, which two days can you put aside for this? This took us somewhat aback but we ended up having a wonderful time visiting almost every section of the hospital from the laundry room to special care units, talking to people and looking at an amazing number of Christmas trees (around 40) which had been made up by members of staff in their own time then choosing the winner. A truly memorable occasion

But who was unhappy over Christmas? We had great pleasure in attending a number of carol services, one of the most moving being that at HM Prison Sudbury on 14th December. This is an open prison in quite pleasant surroundings with no high walls and grim outlook like Stafford jail down the road. It is full of long-term prisoners of reasonable character who have nearly served out their time. They often work outside in the area on all sorts of jobs and have generally a good reputation for being helpful within the community. However, with prisons as crowded as they are at present, sometimes prisoners get sent to Sudbury who would be better off elsewhere. The governor who has no control of this was a pleasant fellow. From his point of view every time one of the inmates walks out of his prison he can do nothing whatsoever about it except to make a report which is of course public. It is a stupid thing for a prisoner to do because on return he is sent back to a high security jail. The week before Christmas unfortunately a number of these incidents had occurred and much had been made of it in the local press.

Upon meeting the governor on this occasion it was sympathy and cheering up he required as well as a sincere wish for a Happy Christmas.

Chapter 14

IN MEMORIAM

Memorial Service to Sir Stanley Clarke

Much has been said about Sir Stanley Clarke but above all, although he was a national figure, he always remained a Staffordshire man who always vigorously supported initiatives within the county which he considered worthwhile. For instance for us in Burton the Rotary Club's cancer ward fund for Queen's Hospital and the racecourse in Uttoxeter which he improved to a national scale are well known. His work and support for Lichfield Cathedral however was not generally so well known, his tireless attendance at many events when he was High Sheriff (complete always with the sword) and so on; others have paid tributes much better I am able.

His memorial service was moving, the cathedral was packed with many people who knew him and sometime worked for him; most will remember the very touching and human account given by his family especially his grand-daughters. I was honoured indeed to represent East Staffordshire on this sad but memorable occasion.

Funeral of policemen killed on duty

This was possibly the most moving event we attended during our year in office. The service was held in Lichfield Cathedral following the death on duty of Detective Constable Michael Swindells. This came under our jurisdiction as, although the incident took place in Birmingham, he was living at the time in Branston. The cathedral was packed with police personnel from his division. In answer to our question every policeman present (and there must have been several hundred) had been replaced by stand-ins from other divisions. There were many other VIPs present. This was followed by cremation at Bretby and a wake at Coors visitor centre. A very suitable tribute following a most tragic event.

Afterword

THE MOST MEMORABLE EVENT

Question – David of all the experiences in engineering and nearly 450 different events many of which are mentioned in this book, which gave you the most real satisfaction?

Reply – There are many which well qualify for second place – after a three year project turning improved drinking water on to nearly 1 million people at Melbourne, visit of Princess Royal to JCB, secret design work on the millennium monument in Uttoxeter and succeeding against all odds, concerts in our Main Hall at Burton with the Wurlitzer, the royal garden party, visits to our volunteers, those wonderful old soldiers in the British Legion and Suez veterans, maybe just being elected councillor and so on but there is one which gave me somehow that inner glow especially on the way back on a wintery night on 11th March. Some preamble first:

As a youngster my father took my brother and I to see Nottingham Forest or Leicester City way back in the late 50's. To see Arther Rowley slotting them in from outside the penalty area was pure magic but soon I was away as a student and starting to play hockey on Saturday afternoons which I also much enjoyed. When it came to my turn as a father in the late 70s when our two boys were old enough the hooliganism, aggression, unfunny obscene language and element of danger frankly put me off taking the boys to watch a match.

That was where it stood until as a very new raw councillor I was very kindly invited by Ben Robinson to see the Albion play, which again I thoroughly enjoyed. For me to meet Nigel Clough before the game was a really great experience and quite over the top. I was impressed by the old ground, it had a certain intimacy and friendliness about it. You could pick out people you knew and as a special bonus listen to Brian Clough's comments loudly expressed from his special seat in the stand. I realised invariably what he said was both packed with knowledge of the finer arts of football and very pertinent but also, most embarrassing of all, completely beyond my understanding.

I thought of the club in terms of that special something it was giving for around 10,000 old Burtonians wherever they were very Saturday week in, week out. They might be too old now to see the match or too far away to go themselves but they could always hide behind the Mail on a Saturday evening (to keep out the ladies) whilst giving proper attention to 'how the Brewers got on.'

When the matter of a move to the Pirelli ground came up I could see good reasons for this in terms of better facilities all round (which I saw later included changing facilities for lady referees) and a chance for them in time even to play in the Football League. This was exciting but I could see from reports and guesswork that financially it was most likely on a knife edge, especially if onerous unnecessary conditions were imposed from outside. Then at a Planning Committee shortly after when the County Council were wanting a huge sum for a new access island, clearly only basically required for four hours once every two weeks in the winter months, I felt this might very likely, together with some other conditions I was not too happy with regarding the timing of the housing development on the old site, jeopardise the whole project.

After all this was for the people of Burton. I found myself nearest to 'losing my cool' for the first time in the four years I had served on the committee. I kept on thinking of those old boys who were no doubt telling their friends that it would never happen; and they would be right wouldn't they?

Then (at last) I come to that AGM. When we arrived (that's me and John the chauffeur) the room was already packed with just one seat at the very front. I had intended to listen from the back and give some quiet words of encouragement when appropriate, but no chance of that.

They went through the usual agenda and I looked around watching carefully particularly the club directors sitting round a table on the stage at the front.

Ben Robinson was explaining how they were getting more from Fairclough Homes for the old ground, more from sponsorship deals between themselves and Pirelli, and more from the Stadium Improvement Fund also praising the County Council and the Football Licensing Authority saying that they 'were extremely impressed by the project.'

What made this event so special for me came just then. With the money problems they had (which I suspected were being downplayed) only real determination to succeed on the part of the Chairman plus overall support from the board as a whole was vital for success. The Chairman clearly had this. It was when I looked round at the board, fairly elderly men probably each with little or no knowledge of a project such as this, but with a job they had done for years with long records of support and loyalty to the Albion, I believed just then they would all do their bit to help as far as they were able and they would succeed.

I then had no hesitation in praising them for their courage and foresight in building the new stadium and looking forward to a real red letter day for the town when it opened.

Later as we all know the project was completed and together with some degree of luck, mainly due to 'FA Cup balls in a bag,' they not only succeeded but took most of the town over to Manchester to the hallowed turf of Old Trafford.